ODIAC SYM.
Its Charm, Beauty, and Fascination

PLATE I: Aries, see symbology on page 39

PLATE II: Taurus, see symbology on page 43

ODIAC SYMBOLOGY
Its Charm, Beauty, and Fascination

Faith Javane
with
Joan Tilden, Research Assistant

Whitford Press

1469 Morstein Road
West Chester, Pennsylvania 19380 USA

PLATE III: Gemini, see symbology on page 47

PLATE IV: Cancer, see symbology on page 51

This book is for everyone who has a birthday.

Published by WHITFORD PRESS
A division of
Schiffer Publishing, Ltd.
1469 Morstein Road
West Chester, Pennsylvania 19380
Please write for a free catalog.
This book may be purchased from the publisher.
Please include $2.00 postage.
Try your bookstore first.

ACKNOWLEDGMENTS

A book is rarely written in isolation, and I have been fortunate to have the assistance of several special people in this project.

I am grateful to Edith L. Craig for her invaluable assistance in the preparation of this book.

I thank Linda Stead for her continued confidence in me and my work.

I appreciate the skill of my editor, Shawn C. Harriman.

And above all, I know that this project has maintained my high standards and been made much more enjoyable because of the participation of my research assistant Joan Tilden. Her enthusiastic and steadfast presence, combined with her careful research, beautiful artwork and cover design, and meticulous graphics, has proven to be a major contribution to this book, and I shall always consider her work with love and gratitude.

PLATE V: Leo, see symbology on page 55

PLATE VI: Virgo, see symbology on page 59

CONTENTS

PART THREE: FURTHER TRADITIONAL ZODIAC SYMBOLOGY

PLATE VII: Libra, see symbology on page 63

PLATE VIII: Scorpio, see symbology on page 67

PART ONE:
INTRODUCTION

FOREWORD

The story of this book and of the Zodiacal paintings it features begins many years ago.

I began my study of Astrology about fifty years ago. At that time I was part of a small study group of neighbors and friends that met to discuss informally our more formal lessons.

Some of our discussions came to focus upon the Elements—Fire, Earth, Air, and Water. We came to appreciate that these Elements were not simply chemical substances but also, and more importantly, *symbolic* subdivisions of the matter. Fire symbolizes spiritual energy moving in spirals. Earth is the symbolic virgin Element, the natural matrix. Air stands for that which permits the circulation of all substances. And Water represents the "seed" of all things, and—in that humanity is a seed of God—the secret vitality of humanity.

The Elements became for my study group an important aid in understanding the Signs of the Zodiac on a deeper level. One member of the group was Miriam Mason Cutting, a psychic visionary artist. Applying our newly-gained insights into the Signs as perceived through the Elements, Miriam sketched her conceptions of each Sign, as follows.

PLATE IX: Sagittarius, see symbology on page 71

PLATE X: Capricorn, see symbology on page 75

The Fire Signs

ARIES   "A Torch Bearer"

Seen as a flame of fire, uncontrolled, a signal of strength and power raised aloft to light the "way" unto others.

LEO   "The Illumined Cross Above the Earth"

Depicted as the fiery, radiant energy of the Sun, the background for the Solar center of the Zodiacal System.

SAGITTARIUS   "The Winged Horns Of Plenty As Blessings"

Filled with violets and roses, symbols of spiritual love and faithfulness, forever within the golden glow of the tamed fire of Spirit.

The Earth Signs

TAURUS   "Rockbound Gates Spanned By The Rainbow"

Suggestive of solitude and meditative radiance. The rainbow is a phenomenon of our earthly promise in brotherhood and harmony.

VIRGO   "The Growing Vine With Fronds Unfolding"

Implies hidden growth beneath the surface, culminating in knowledge, reason, and Truth.

CAPRICORN   "The Vine-Clad Rock Of Ages"

Envisioned as reassuring us that even upon the rocky cliffs there is sustenance and growth which creates within us the challenge to climb and behold the view.

The Air Signs

GEMINI   "The Winged Caduceus With Violet Flame"

A spiritual energy bearing knowledge and understanding. Dual in

Source, although opposite in color, the helping hands are for the good of all humanity.

LIBRA "Rainbow Of Beauty And Art, Prism Of Light"

Pictured as radiating from the Sun and Crescent Moon in polarity, spilling over the receptive Earth awaiting its bounty.

AQUARIUS "Downpouring Of Spirit Over The Earth"

Depicted as a vast waterfall from the Cosmic spreading the liquid golden essence of Divine Light to the understanding heart of Love and Truth.

The Water Signs

CANCER "Beacon Light Upon The Shoals"

Suggestive of the nurturing characteristic of the great "Mother Sign" Cancer.

SCORPIO "Star Of Heaven And Of The Sea"

The deep blue color used as background for all the Water Signs strongly marks the conception of the depths of emotion throughout the Water Element.

PISCES "Christ In The Mirrored Waters"

The traditional living waters, conceived as water of life and the rainbow of promise. Envisioned as Christ reflected through the rainbow of living waters into the waters-of-life below.

Miriam's work appears as the titles and in the ovals of the current paintings. The philosophical ideals that the group uncovered and that Miriam tuned into are thus an important contribution to the development of this book.

Many years later I became very active in Edgar Cayce's organization, the now well-known Association for Research and Enlightenment, or A.R.E. While attending an A.R.E. seminar at Virginia Beach in the late 1960s, I met Jane Evelyn Murphy, an artist. Returning to the work I

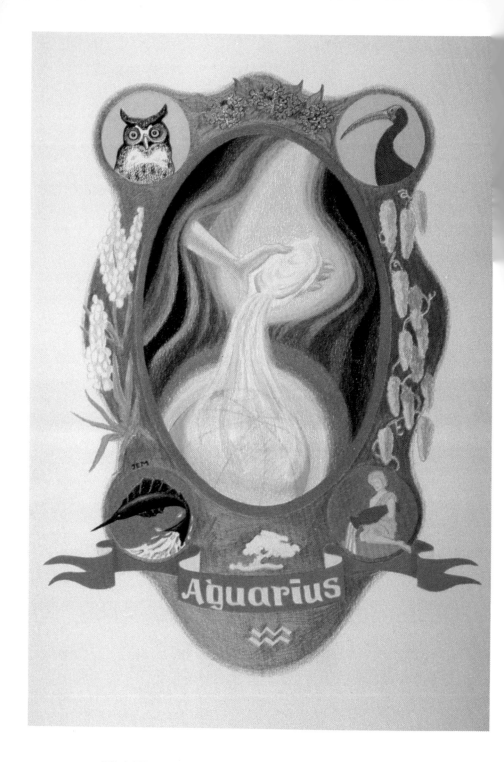

PLATE XI: Aquarius, see symbology on page 79

PLATE XII: Pisces, see symbology on page 83

had begun with Miriam, I provided Jane with extensive information I had since researched for each Sign. I then commissioned Jane to complete the painting around Miriam's original ovals based on the information I had given her.

Since then, I have used these paintings often in my lecturing and teaching activities. But I have also always wanted to share these lovely studies of Zodiac symbology with an ever-wider audience. I have considered presenting the paintings as birthday greeting cards, in a brief souvenir booklet, or even as a perpetual calendar.

In the end, my desire has taken the shape of a book, as I accompanied the paintings with more detailed yet still accessible information culled from many volumes of notes I have taken over the years. I was aided in this research by my dear friend and former student Joan Tilden, and we believe that an orientation to astrology, an explanation of the symbols in the paintings, and some mention of the rich heritage of other Zodiacal symbols will best serve those who look to the metaphysical arts to understand themselves and others.

May, then, this book assist you as you seek to discover the wisdom which is ever surrounding us in our journey through the Earth Plane!

Faith Javane
Dover, New Hampshire

INTRODUCTION

We are all called to make clear decisions in our lives; to do so successfully, we must know our own minds as well as listen to the counsel of others. Although we should be adaptable, in the end we decide for ourselves. We then discover that all knowledge and guidance actually lies within us; we realize that there exists in us a "center" where Truth is known and realized in totality.

> "Truth is within ourselves _____
> Whate'er you may believe, there is
> an *inmost center* in us all where
> Truth abides in fullness—whence
> the Imprisoned Splendor may escape
> effecting entry for a Light
> supposed to be *without*."

from Robert Brownings's *Paracelsus*

There also exist many external "signboards" to guide us in our search for the knowledge within us. These signboards are found in the study of metaphysics, and include such techniques as the reading of our Akashic Records, our Numerological delineations,[1] and our Horoscopes, or Astrological Charts.

---

[1] Consult *Numerology and the Divine Triangle* by Faith Javane and Dusty Bunker (West Chester, PA: Whitford Press, 1979).

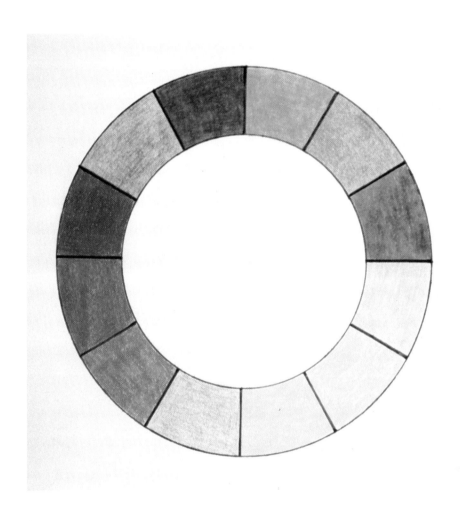

PLATE XIII: Rainbow of the Zodiac, see page 100

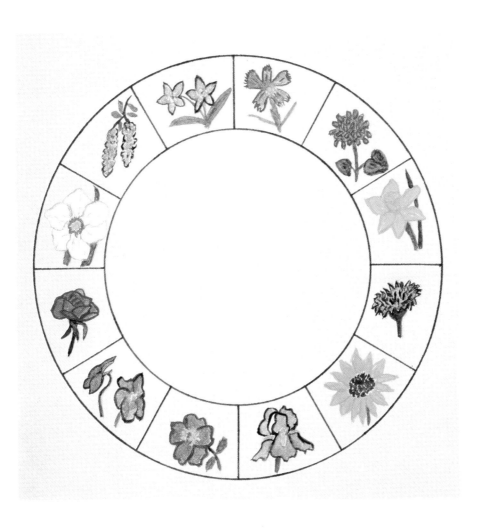

PLATE XIV: Flowers of the Zodiac.

The preparation and analysis of an Astrological Chart can help us obtain both practical information about how to live our daily lives as well as thoughtful insights into the mysteries of the Universe. Wise men and women and humble folk alike have furthered the evolution of humanity by the study of astrology in both its mundane and esoteric expressions. Astrology can help us to comprehend vibratory forces and to change them to suit our changing consciousness. Thus can knowledge evolve into wisdom and thus can intellect raise our spirits from the world of dense matter to the Kingdom of Light.

Symbols are another important "signboard" for our journeys. Symbols may serve to open us to that "still, small voice" which is the Divine Center within us. All flowers, trees, and herbs have their own Symbology and vibratory rates, as do gems and incense and perfumes. Birds and animals have their Symbology, too. Even in the world of chemistry and metallurgy there exist rays of harmony or discord.

This book is intended to give an unbiased presentation covering the connections between Symbology and Astrology in a holistic and elevated manner. I make no absolute claims about relationships between Signs and Symbols, but I have attempted to present clear and relevant material in an Interesting fashion. I hope to have been eclectic, open-minded, and sound in tone, to have presented information from a humanistic and spiritual perspective, and to have been lucid yet original in temperament.

This book is not a book for the Astrological specialist (although even she or he may find it a useful reference source). I do not present the entire study of Astrology, but rather only its major symbolic aspects and that which can be generally accepted by the average reader.

Thus, on whatever level this book is read, I confidently pray that it will provide some insight into our individual destinies and on the human condition in general.

1

THE SKY

The starry sky, in its nebulous and opalescent beauty, creates in us a fascination that drives us to explore its mysteries. The constellations in the sky, and the streams of energy which pass and re-pass, intermingle, and interlock throughout all space express the vibratory forces of creation, forces which powerfully influence our daily lives and destinies.

The extent of creation as we know it is called the Universe. The Universe is made up of very large groups of stars called Galaxies. Galaxies come in three main shapes—spiral, elliptical, and irregular—and there are approximately 100,000,000 Galaxies throughout the Universe. Our own Galaxy, the Milky Way, is believed to contain about 100,000,000,000 Stars, or Suns, and is 160,000 Light Years in diameter.

Smaller groupings of Stars within a Galaxy are called Constellations. Constellations have been named after animals or mythological figures or other earthly objects (see chapter 2), but often the shapes of the Constellations today look nothing like their names. This is because in the thousands of years since the Constellations were first named, everything in the Universe has been moving, expanding away from the point of creation, and the Stars have moved and pulled the former "star-pictures" out of shape. For example, Ursa Major, the Great Bear, looks much more like an old-fashioned long-handled dipper than a bear, hence its popular name, the Big Dipper.

The Universe is commonly depicted as a globe, with the Earth considered the center of the sphere. (Of course, the Earth is not the center of the Universe, and this representation is simply one of convenience.) Maps of the Universe are based on this globe; a complete picture of the heavens consists of two circular maps showing the north and south hemispheres of the Universe globe.

At the North Pole of this Universe globe is the Pole Star. Because the Earth, as part of this Solar System and the Milky Way Galaxy, moves through the heavens over time, the Pole Star actually changes. In 3000 B.C. the bright Star Thuban in the Constellation Draco was recorded as the Pole Star. The current Pole Star is Polaris. Astronomers have calculated that by 5000 A.D. the Star Gamma in the Constellation Cepheus will be over the North Pole, and by 14,000 A.D. the Pole Star will be Vega, a bright Star in the Constellation Lyra. By 25,000 A.D., Thuban will return to its position as Pole Star.

A map of the Universe is commonly divided into twelve sectors of thirty degrees each. It is these sectors that make up the twelve sectors of an individual's horoscope. In each sector lies the Constellation that names the sector as a Zodiacal Sign, with each Sign representing a certain pattern of personal attributes, as follows.[1]

ARIES
♈
- the desire to rise and rule, leadership and pioneering, great magnetism

TAURUS
♉
- the builder with determination and stability, interest in financial retention, productivity and sustenance

GEMINI
♓
- intellectual interest in art and science, writing ability, inventive and self-expressive

CANCER
♋
- self-consciousness, shaping of inner soulic and outer physical natures, planning and preparation, performance of duty

LEO
♌
- eloquence, enthusiasm, energy, revelry in sensory perception

VIRGO
♍
- analytical, practical, resourceful, healthful, conservative in action

---

[1] For more detailed descriptions, consult a basic astrology text.

THE ZODIAC IN THE SKY

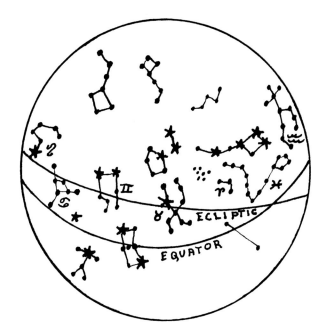

North and South Hemispheres

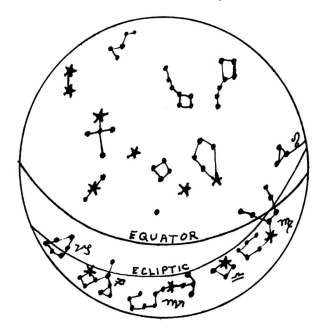

★ Denotes Fixed Stars

LIBRA
♎ — equilibrium and justice, social success, partnership with tact and diplomacy

SCORPIO
♏ — generation, re-generation, or de-generation

SAGITTARIUS
♐ — inspirational, philosophical, and spiritual

CAPRICORN
♃ — honor-seeking, ambition, conservative and economical

AQUARIUS
♒ — the power of knowledge poured out for all to see

PISCES
♓ — super-physical sensitivity, mystical and illusionary experiences becoming pertinent to the normal happenings of life, the ability to have two kinds of experience simultaneously

These twelve Constellations are found on the Universe map close to the Ecliptic, a circular path on the map near the Equator. Because, however, of the unbounded expansion of the Universe, some of the Constellations today overlap into adjoining sectors.

Many Constellations besides the Sign's designated Constellation symbolize conditions to that Sign. These Constellations, some of which expand outward across several Signs, are powerful forces in the Universe, and can play an important role in one's astrological chart. A listing of selected influential Constellations, along with their vibratory significance, follows.[2]

ARIES
Triagulum—a trinity, indicating a union of mind, body, and spirit, which shows the importance of cooperation
Eridanus—the elixir of life, perpetual youth, power attained through development of love
Perseus—believer that progressive thought stamps out materialism

TAURUS
Lepus, the Hare—the requirement to overcome timidity

---
[2] For more detail and clarification consult a good astronomy text.

and materialism
  Orion, the Mighty Hunter—struggle or mental combat between
    spirituality and materialism
  Auriga, the Charioteer—seen as protecting the weak, thereby
    gaining in spirituality

GEMINI

  Ursa Minor, the Small Bear—influencing the subconscious mind as
    a voice of silence
  Canis Major, the Big Dog—writing and speaking skills, service to
    higher mind
  Ursa Major, the Great Bear—capacity for thought, idealism, and
    faith; the conscious will, the rise of conscious experience in the
    soul

CANCER

  Canis Minor, the Little Dog—the need to develop poise and
    faithfulness
  Hydra, the Water Serpent—the struggle to confront desires of
    dramatic tendencies
  Argo, the Ship—the tendency to seek out the secrets of nature and
    the occult

LEO

  Crater—powerful, fiery love nature, the need for moderation and
    control
  Centaurus, Half Horse and Half Man—adaptability, the need for
    restraint from dictatorial tendencies
  Corvus, the Raven—the desire for authority

VIRGO

  Bootes, the Driver—harvest of life's wine and grain
  Hercules, the Hero—the ability to accomplish great things for
    humanity
  Coronoa Borealis, the Northern Crown—soul gains won by hard
    work

LIBRA

  Serpens—creative energy, the ability to guide others, conjugality,
    judicial acumen and keenness
  Draco, the Dragon—originality for changing the "old order"

Lupus, the Wolf—power and usefulness through developed higher inspiration

SCORPIO

Orphiucus, the Wrestler—the struggle with one's emotions, the need to guide energy to bring out higher vibrations

The Altar—vivid and abundant physical force which must be keyed to duty, investigation, and research

Corona Australis, the Southern Crown—revelation that generative potency when sublimated may carry the soul to lofty heights

SAGITTARIUS

Lyra, the Seven-Stringed Harp—attunement to the Infinite, following the inner voice

Aquilla, the Eagle—the higher mind making lofty flights through the astral

Sapgitta, the Arrow—the soul piercing the illusions of matter

CAPRICORN

Cygnus, the Swan—a new order, safety and dignity

Delphinus, the Dolphin—working about the material that brings capability for self-sacrifice in the interests of universal evolution

Pisces Australis, the Southern Fish-performance of public service, the possibility of astral communication through higher emotional activity

AQUARIUS

Pegasus, the Flying Horse—the carrying of spiritual knowledge for all to gain

Cetus, the Whale—the devouring of those who practice materialism instead of altruism

Equuleus, the Colt—power of mind, knowledge of human nature, and universal love

PISCES

Cepheus, the King—the search for truth among dreams

Andromeda, the Chained Princess—the Earth-bound condition of the human soul

Cassiopea, the Queen—the binding of psychic faculties through misuse of sensitive urges, nullified through redemption

To construct the Horoscope, we take the twelve Zodiacal Signs out of the Universe map and draw a circle of the Signs, with ARIES, the first sign, at the right ascending meridian.

THE ZODIACAL CONSTELLATIONS

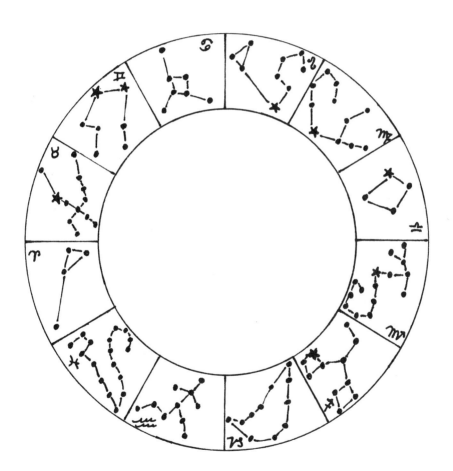

Depending upon the time of birth, other astronomical elements, particularly the Planets but also fixed stars[3] and asteroids, fall in a unique combination of Signs. The Planets are associated with spiritual energies, and in ancient times were considered to represent gods and goddesses according to those deities's generally accepted characteristics. These identities seemed to indicate that intelligences from higher planes could communicate back and forth with those on the earth plane (see chapter 2).

Throughout one's life, the Planets will move through the various Signs of the Horoscopes, as indicated in an individual's progressed astrological chart. Astrology is the study of individual Horoscopes to help determine the relationship between the forces operating in the Universe (as indicated by the Constellations and Planets) and the lives and evolution of individual men and women.

A number of new astronomical discoveries are also influencing the shape of Horoscopes. As new Planets have been discovered, they have assumed rulership over different Houses, or sectors of the Horoscopes. Further Planetary discoveries are expected, and eventually there will be twelve Planets, one for each Sign.

Currently, researchers are also studying several asteroids, or planetoids, for their influences on horoscopes. A selection is given here:

Ceres ⚳

Ceres relates to nurturing on all levels, and brings productive and service-oriented vibrations.

Chiron ⚷

The best-known of the asteroids, Chiron's position in one's chart (House, Sign, etc.) can indicate the nature and terms of one's life-quest.

Juno ⚵

Juno signifies charm, strength in marriage and partnerships, and diplomatic skills.

Pallas ⚴

Pallas concerns the teaching of justice for humanity, and carries inventive and determined qualities.

---

[3] Faith Javane, *Our Stars of Destiny* (1988) West Chester, PA: Whitford Press, pp. 161-163.

Persephone

Persephone is thought to relate to rebirth, the breaking through the illusion and fear of death, connections with nature, and earthly wisdom. Its existence has been predicted mathematically but has not actually been sighted yet because of its enormous distance away from the Earth.

Vesta

Vesta involves dedication to career.

The continued quest for knowledge about the sky, as epitomized by the recent launching of the great Hubble Telescope, will undoubtedly reveal many further wonders, which will guide us in our search for self-knowledge and self-betterment. The appearance of new Planets and planetoids in the heavens is considered to measure the expansion of human consciousness. These celestial bodies are hidden from humanity because of its low level of evolution. The discovery of a new object expands the powers available to individuals seeking to evolve to higher levels of consciousness. Such a discovery and the research on the objects meanings for and influences on human life should permit us to experiment with new concepts and types of outreach. Humanity must change its rigid rules as often as necessary to match current conditions, with the new patterns pointing always in the direction of the Divine Plan—that of attaining the goal of Cosmic Consciousness.

2

THE HISTORY OF THE
ZODIAC AND ASTROLOGY

"All the stars and constellations were appointed to be rulers and commandants over the world ... There is not a single blade of grass in the entire world over which a star or a planet does not preside."

The Zohar[1]

Astrology is the science that studies the relationship between us and these forces, expressed in the Zodiacal constellations (the Signs) and the Planets. The word "astrology" means "star wisdom," and, in the words of Ralph Waldo Emerson, "astrology is astronomy brought to earth and applied to the affairs of men." All civilizations have included astrology among their sciences and philosophies, and each civilization has contributed to the advancement of the discipline.

What is the meaning of the Signs of the Zodiac? A Sign is a symbol, something that carries a message, and humanity has always asked itself what the messages in the sky mean. Yet knowledge of astrology has always been present; no search of the histories of China, India, Babylon, Egypt, Greece, or Rome has uncovered a time when the constellations were un-named, or when the meanings of these constellations were unknown. And, as already noted, the names for the constellations bear little or no resemblance to their recent shapes.

---

[1] The Zohar—a 14th-century kabbalistic treatise.

The constellations thus seem to have been fixed in the heavens by some unquestionable authority for untold eons.

The answer to the mystery of who fixed the constellations thus can be found in the Book of the Secrets of Enoch, an ancient sacred book excluded from our present Bible. Although written down at the beginning of the Christian era, the Book of Enoch records events from the very dawn of humanity's evolution.

It is not clear who exactly Enoch was, or where he lived. Although many traditions place him in the Biblical Old Testament tradition or at the time of the Egyptian mystery schools, it is likely that he lived in even earlier days, and lived not in the Middle or Near East but rather the Far East. Legends call Enoch the father of astrology, and attribute to him the teaching of arts and laws, the inventions of writings and books, and, perhaps most importantly, discovery of the knowledge of the Zodiac and the course of the Planets. The Book of Enoch details how Enoch learned the mysteries of the skies, and names God Himself as the entity who named the Signs and who described their influences on humanity, thus arranging the Signs to set forth His plan for creation.

In the time of Enoch, religion was in a very primitive state. Filled with superstition, people then perceived all the workings of nature as the result of invisible powers. These superhuman powers controlled human destiny through miracles, magic, and both good and evil spirits and forces. The earth was the center of the universe, with the Sun and Planets orbiting around it. Heaven was above, and the abode of the "wicked" was below.

Enoch was visited one day by two angels, who took him on their wings and showed him the Heavens above the Earth. The Heavens were divided into ten levels. In the First, Second, and Third Heaven, the angels showed Enoch the far reaches of the Earth and all of creation.

In the Fourth Heaven (chapter 11 in the Book of Enoch), the angels showed him "all the rays of light of the Sun and Moon, the circle and the wheel on which they go." They brought him to the east to the Sun's gate "where the Sun goes forth according to the regulation of the seasons and the circuit of the months of the whole year, and the numbers of the hours of day and night." They also brought him to the west, where the Sun sets, and to the course of the Moon, "twelve great gates (the months) by which the moon goes in and out."

In the Fifth Heaven the angels told Enoch the story of "Satanail," who was sent from Heaven with his followers. The Sixth Heaven was the abode of the archangels "who are appointed over seasons and years." The Seventh Heaven was a place of great light, of dominion and government, of cherubim and seraphim. In the Eighth Heaven, Enoch saw the twelve Signs of the Zodiac, and the Ninth Heaven was the home of the Signs.

The Tenth Heaven was the House of God, and Enoch came face to face with God Himself. God spoke to Enoch and revealed to him many secrets. God told him, "Enoch, beloved, all thou seest, all that are standing finished I tell to thee even before the very beginning, all that I created from nonbeing, and visible things from invisible" (Enoch 24:1). God described the days of the creation, similar to the creation account in the Book of Genesis. On the fourth day, God created "the Sun that it should go according to each animal (Zodiacal Sign) twelve, and I appointed the succession of the months and their names" (Enoch 30:6).

The remainder of the Book of Enoch contains various instructions, warnings, and prophecies of the future. As Enoch prepares to depart from the Heavens, God charges him, "Apply thy mind, Enoch, and know who is speaking to thee, and take thou the books which thou thyself hast written ... go down to Earth, and tell thy sons all that I have told thee, and all that thou hast seen, from the lower heaven up to My throne ... Give them the books ... and they will read them, and will know Me for the creator of all things, and will understand that there is no other God but Me ... and let them distribute the books ... generation to generation, nation to nation" (Enoch 33:6-10).

Thus was revealed to humanity the names of the constellations or Signs and their significance. This knowledge was often lost or obscured, but we can trace a history of astrology from the East and uncover its circuitous trek into the Western tradition.

Among the earliest civilizations were those that flourished in Southeast Asia and China. We do not always recognize how very advanced they were. The Chinese understood the workings of right-angle triangles five centuries before the Greeks "discovered" the theorems of geometry and Pythagoras demonstrated his theorem. The Chinese were also quite sophisticated astronomers, and recorded comets and eclipses early in their history. We find astrological notations in the most ancient records of China.

Religion and astrology soon spread from Eastern Asia to India. There, religion developed from a relatively primitive state basically consisting of the simple veneration of nature into a more elaborate system based on both mystical and rational elements. Indian sacred and scientific teachings were handed down for centuries only by mouth; thus, the knowledge eventually written in the already ancient Vedic scriptures has a particularly early origin. The Vedas contain a number of astronomical calculations, and related astrological tables are nearly as old. Although Hindu astrology was kept and passed on only through priests of the Brahmin caste, the knowledge of astrology in Indian society was relatively widespread.

From India, this knowledge moved to Chaldea (Babylon) and to Egypt. In Chaldea, developments seemed to focus more on the scientific and astronomical knowledge and its applications for agriculture, politics, and religion, while in Egypt the knowledge became appropriated by the temple priests and shrouded in mystery.

The Chaldeans codified the beginnings of the system of Zodiacal Signs used today. Chaldean astrologers fixed the constellations so that the solstices and equinoxes were on the first, fourth, seventh, and tenth cusps of the Zodiac, with Aries the ram as the first Sign. The first calendar was also developed from this fixing of the Zodiac. Two hours were allotted to each Sign, giving a twenty-four-hour day beginning at midnight. Each Sign also represented one month, and the year's four seasons were set as follows, with each season consisting of three Signs:

Spring:	Aries, Taurus, Gemini
Summer:	Cancer, Leo, Virgo
Fall:	Libra, Scorpio, Sagittarius
Winter:	Capricorn, Aquarius, Pisces

A year was defined as the time it took the Sun to make a complete circuit of the Zodiac.

The priests of Egypt gathered their vast knowledge from sources in India as well as from Chaldea, Persia, Syria, Arabia, and Phoenicia. Among the early great figures of Egyptian religion was Thoth, also called Hermes Trismegistus or Mercury. Thoth instructed the initiated temple priests in a secret body of knowledge from India. This information was guarded very carefully by the priesthood over the centuries, thus keeping from the masses the knowledge God had originally given to Enoch and intended for all people. The priests compiled this hidden knowledge into great books on the occult and hermetic sciences and augmented these teachings with discoveries and revelations of their own. In particular, the priests established festivals for sacrifices to the Sun under each of the Zodiacal Signs.

Astrological knowledge was recorded by Ptolemy in his great book the *Tetrabiblios* and in his *Almagest*, the first almanac, which included the earliest record of star magnitudes. Egyptian astrology had only ten Signs.

The religious and astrological heritage of the Hebrews traces back to both Chaldean and Egyptian roots. The Old Testament abounds in astrological symbology and teaching, and the Hebrew prophets developed a clear intuitive rapport with the workings of the heavens. In the Book of Job, God reveals his power and states that the heavens can provide prophecy, purpose, and counsel to humanity. The Book of Job also mentiones the Pleiades, Arcturus, and Orion, as well as the Mazzeroth, the Biblical term for the Zodiac (Job 38:1-3). The Book of Ecclesiastes demonstrates the Hebrew understanding of the relationship between the ordering of the sky and human endeavors: "To everything there is a season, and a time to every purpose under the heavens ... for there is a time for every ... work" (Ecclesiastes 3:1, 17). Finally, in the Book of Psalms we find one of the more well-known and eloquent passages about the place of the Zodiac in God's plan; indeed, the psalm in question has been called "The Astrologer's Psalm."

"The heavens declare the glory of God; and the firmament sheweth his handiwork. Day unto day uttereth speech, and night unto night sheweth knowledge. There is not speech nor language where their voice is not heard. Their line has gone out through all the earth, and the words to the end of the world."

Psalm 19:1-4

The ancient Greeks were the next main group to advance humanity's knowledge of religion and astrology. Their contributions reveal the Greeks' great concern with developing a philosophy that related man's spirit to his physical environment and Nature. Obviously, the cosmos and the Zodiac played an important role in much of this development. In 460 B.C. Hippocrates wrote that those studying medicine must know every herb and tree and their relation to the Zodiacal Signs. He believed that the planetary positions and aspects in individuals' horoscopes would indicate their condition and the proper herbal cure. Eudoxus, a Greek astronomer, (ca. 4,000 B.C.), played a major role in organizing the Zodiac with his work on constellations, stars of greater magnitude, and mathematical and geometrical models based on the cosmos, its solstitial patterns, and its circles the ecliptic, the equator, and the tropics. In 120 B.C. Hipparchus mapped the sky into forty-eight constellations, adding to earlier-named constellations ones named for prominent Greek leaders like Perseus and Hercules. These people were admired and idolized for their strength and courage, and were favored by the Gods, being made heroes or demi-gods. The Greeks also increased the number of Signs of the Zodiac, adding Libra between Virgo and Scorpio.

Along with major progress in astronomy and astrology, the Greeks significantly expanded the sophistication of spiritual thought as well as its linkages with scientific knowledge. Among the many important Greeks scientists and thinkers who contributed advances in religious and philosophical thought were the following'

Pythagoras (ca. 600 B.C.) stated that souls are spirits imprisoned in material bodies, and that numbers symbolize important and permanent truths

Anaxagoras (ca. 500 B.C.)—taught that One Mind ordered matter

Heraclitus (ca. 490 B.C.)—believed that the Earth was formed by a fiery, all-penetrating element of which souls were a part

Socrates (ca. 470 B.C.)—studied human virtue, particularly prudence, courage, self-control, and justice

Plato (ca. 427 B.C., student of Socrates)—believed in immortal souls that "knew" through previous experience

Aristotle (ca. 384 B.C., student of Plato)—wrote that human beings were composed both of a body and a soul but also a divine spark, the logos, which is eternal though impersonal and shared with God

The world of medieval Europe relied heavily on the ideas of the ancient Greeks, and indeed medieval times are often misconstrued as "the Dark Ages." In reality, much study and research on metaphysical matters took place, albeit often in remote areas or in secret or limited circumstances. Many treatises still survive from these times, on such varied topics as Christian and Jewish mysticism, alchemy, herbal lore, astrology and the Tarot, the Kabbalah, the lives of saints, prayer and meditation, philosophy and science, and other related matters. Paracelsus (ca. 1493), the great philosopher and physician of the late Middle Ages, taught that everything that exists has underlying hidden principles and relationships with other things. He also believed that people live in sympathetic relation to the constellations, and he was particularly known for his research upon the connection between stars and plants, especially herbs, and the connection between them and the physical body. He learned that the remedy for diseases of the visible body are contained in the invisible body which infuses life into the visible. Herbs, the fruit of nature, have important essences that can produce beneficial healing vibrations to assist the workings of the inner body. The following is a chart used in Paracelsus's day of the relationships between bodily organs, the planets, and herbs.

Organ	Planet	Herbs related to Planet
Heart	Sun	rosemary, lavender, sage, balm
Brain	Moon	rue, wild thyme, black hellebore, Indian poke
Gall Bladder	Mars	nettles, spotted thistle, bitter herb
Kidneys	Venus	mullein, parsley, absinthe, wormwood
Lungs	Mercury	althea, plantain, lung-wort, marsh-mallow
Liver	Jupiter	Indian hemp, liver-wort, rue, maiden fern
Spleen	Saturn	fig-wort, wood-sage, heal-all

As the Middle Ages gave way to the Renaissance and modern times, progress in astrology was based more upon new scientific knowledge than upon specifically religious concerns. In the sixteenth century, Copernicus revived the heliocentric (sun-centered) theory, opposing the geocentric notions of earlier days that stated that the earth was the center of the solar system. In the late sixteenth and early seventeenth century, Tycho Brahe, Johannes Kepler, and Galileo Galilei all made important contributions in recording celestial motions, refuting the notion of circular planetary orbits in favor of the actual elliptical paths, and in developing the telescope and discovering more moons and other celestial bodies. Indeed, these advances were made only with strong opposition from organized religion, in Europe the Roman Catholic Church.

But the Catholic Church was not in power in England, and in the late seventeenth century great astronomers like Isaac Newton and Edmund Halley made many important contributions to scientific knowledge. The first observatories were built in England around 1675, and British researchers using these facilities discovered many of the laws governing time and space and the various motions and cycles of our solar system. These British discoveries have become the basis of modern astrological measurement and interpretation.

Nearly two centuries after the development of the telescope, Herschel discovered Uranus. Fifty years later came Neptune, and Pluto was discovered in 1930, completing the solar system as currently known. These three Planets assumed their places in the Horoscope, thus greatly increasing the accuracy and subtlety of astrological analysis.

Recent years have shown even further exciting discoveries. From space flight to manned space flight to man on the moon (in 1969), and up to Skylab, the Voyager mission to the outer planets, the Space Shuttle, and the Hubble Telescope (in 1990), our knowledge of the Universe is expanding rapidly. Today researchers are planning space stations and even more detailed exploration of outer space beyond our own Galaxy.

Clearly, we have much to learn about the heavens, and as we do, we shall be able to apply this fresh knowledge to astrology and learn more about ourselves and our place in the Universe. And while the advances in recent centuries have been more material, and while our advanced civilization has focused more upon technology and "hard science," we shall in the fast-approaching Age of Aquarius bring a more balanced and spiritual temperament to our explorations and research.[2] The combination of technical knowledge and a humanitarian, ethical, and spiritual perspective will allow humanity to continue its evolution into higher forms of consciousness. As it has for nearly all of human history, astrology as the interpreter of the heavens will play an important role in our progress along this inevitable and wondrous path.

---

[2] For one example of recent advances in metaphysics, consult *Our Stars of Destiny*, Faith Javane, (1988) West Chester, PA: Whitford Press.

PART TWO:
SYMBOLIC ZODIAC PICTURES

3

A KEY TO THE SYMBOLIC
ZODIAC PICTURES

Each of the next twelve chapters in Part Two presents a Zodiacal Sign, its symbolic depiction in the paintings, a description of its major characteristics, and an explanation of the pictured symbology. Each Sign follows a similar pattern:

Title   A phrase summarizing the picture

Bible Quotation   A Biblical citation that captures the essence
                      or an important feature of the Sign

The Individual   A brief characterization of individuals born
                      under this Sign

Graces   The natural strengths given to individuals in
                      this Sign

Challenges   Tendencies that must be confronted and
                      overcome by individuals in this Sign

Glyph   An explanation of the symbols used in
                      Astrology for this Sign

Ruling Planet	The traits brought to the Sign by its related Planet
Pictured Symbology	A listing of the Gems, Flowers, Trees, Birds, and Animals pictured, with an explanation of their symbolic significance for the Sign

Part Three includes further Sign symbology that has not been included in this book's pictures. An explanation of the general significance of the symbols chosen for the pictures is followed by listings of further examples of the pictured symbols. Additional symbology—Colors, Music, Incense, and Herbs—are also explored for each Sign.

4

ARIES SYMBOLOGY

The Torch Bearer

Raise thy torch to the enlightenment of others, thus driving the hostile shadows of disillusionment ever in retreat. Be ever courageous holding aloft the beacon of faith and truth.

Proverbs 27:1
"Boast not thyself of tomorrow, for thou knowest not what a day may bring forth."

"Adventurous Aries"
Mentally and emotionally, you consider yourself a leader and have a strong desire to rise and rule. You are eager to experience all that life has to offer, and your spirit never says "no." You are a pioneer, always prepared for something new and longing to go where no one has before. You have a magnetic personality which is fiery and sometimes angry and combustible.

Aries Graces:
Ardor, courage, independence, strong will.

Aries Challenges:
Impatience, rashness, impulsiveness, boldness.

ARIES, see **PLATE I** for color.

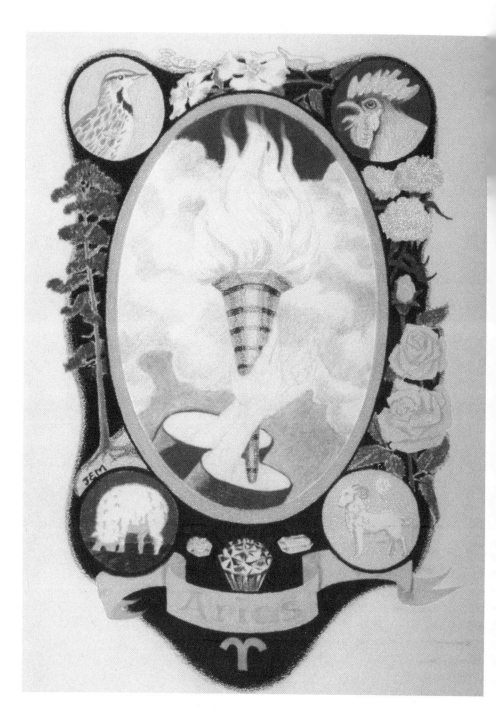

The Glyph: ♈ The Ram
 Represents the head and horns of a ram, or a sprouting seed, or a fountain of water, or a symbol of power.

The Ruling Planet: MARS ♂
 Dynamic energy, drive, aggression, initiative.

Pictured Symbology of ARIES

Gems:
 Diamond: The hardest of all gems, and the most powerful vibrationally. It develops pride and magnifies other gems worn with it.
 Ruby: The gem of courage, a symbol of beauty and elegance. It represents gifts of love, enduring respect, and friendship.
 Tourmaline: Coming in many colors, it is emblematic of harmony among body, soul, and spirit.

Flowers:
 American Beauty Rose: The universal symbol of love.
 Red Carnation: A more ardent or boastful love vibration.

Trees:
 Pine: Valued for resin and other elements, it emanates the red ray of healing.
 Dogwood: Its bark supplies essences of medicinal value, and its blossoms give pleasure from their beauty.

Birds:
 Meadow Lark: Its loud, clear song brings enjoyment when heard as it circles over open fields.
 Cock: Crows as an early alarm of awakening as he struts about claiming his territory.

Animals:
 Entire Sheep Family (expressed as Lamb or Ram): Their heavy wool, edible flesh, and skin for making leather and parchment make them a total aid to humanity.

TAURUS SYMBOLOGY

Rockbound Gates Spanned By The Rainbow

After the tempests of earth cometh the rainbow of promise. On earth, as in heaven, go to the quiet places; seek the solitude to know thyself. Know thy "inner" to be sovereign to the "outer". Beauty of soul becomes beauty of the self; seek to unite the two through faith and truth.

Proverbs 16:3
"Commit your work to the Lord and your place shall be established."

"Thrifty Taurus"
You are a builder and have great determination and stability. You are productive and sustaining and are constructively matter-of-fact. You are concerned with financial conditions and tend to accumulate possessions.

Taurus Graces:
Dependability, patience, self-reliance.

Taurus Challenges:
Possessiveness, materialism, obstinacy, self-indulgence.

TAURUS, see **PLATE II** for color.

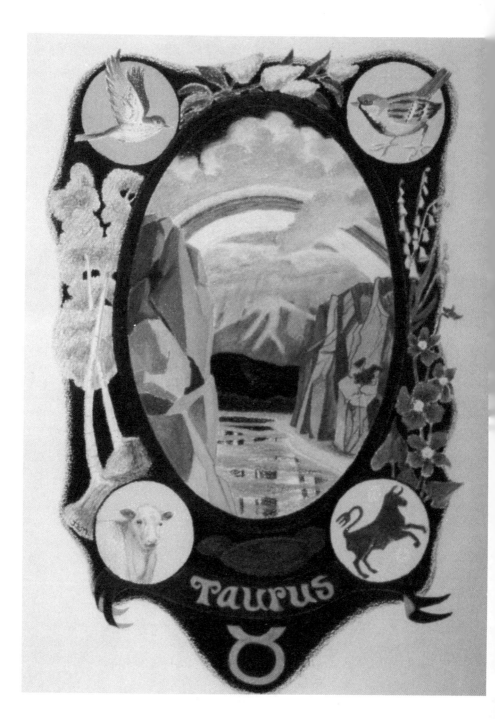

The Glyph: ♉ The Bull
Represents the head and horns of a bull, indicating natural strength and power.

The Ruling Planets: VENUS ♀
Beauty, art, pleasure, capacity to love.

EARTH ⊕
Practicality, common sense.

Pictured Symbology of TAURUS

Gem:
   Emerald: A gem associated with nurturing, patience, and healing, particularly of the eyes. The legendary power of this green stone is to help the wearer judge the true value of self. Also signifies fidelity, success, and happiness.

Flowers:
   Lily-of-the-Valley, Violet: These are shy or modest vibrations, giving sympathy and softness.
   Lilac: The pride of spring.

Tree:
   White Birch: With willow-like branches, its bark was used by the Indians for making canoes.

Birds:
   Dove: A symbol of peace, love, and gentleness.
   Sparrow: A universal bird known for its happy singing.

Animals:
   All Cattle, Oxen and Bulls: Helpful to man as burden bearers, they represent assistance to the inhabitants of the Earth.

6

GEMINI SYMBOLOGY

Winged Caduceus With Violet Flame

Clasp the winged rod and let thy purifying vision unveil the hidden truth and thy spirit approach the Temple Mysteries. Be diligent and active, yet cautious in thy teachings. Seek the wisdom of the Master that thou may do thy Father's Work. Let thy mind's energy penetrate thy soul and manifest it in thy personality. Let not thy short attention span benumb thy perseverance. Patiently concentrate upon effectively delivering God's message intact in truth and love.

Romans 12:2
  "Be ye transformed by the renewing of your mind —-."

"Diversified Gemini"
  You are curious and investigative and use your intellectual powers to realize goals and relationships. You are interested in both art and science and are inventive and self-expressive. You seek to effect unity by demonstrating the unity of cause. You are more humane than domestic, and you have a good commercial sense.

Gemini Graces:
  Versatility, cleverness, adaptability.

GEMINI, see **PLATE III** for color.

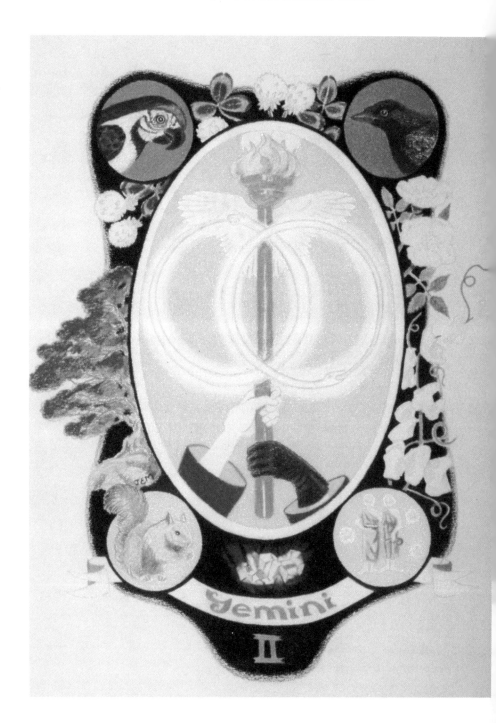

Gemini Challenges:
Fickleness, duality, restlessness.

The Glyph: ♊ The Twins
Represent duality, making right choices, and the rise of conscious will in the soul.

The Ruling Planet: MERCURY ☿
Reason, the mind, educational capacity.

Pictured Symbology of GEMINI

Gem:
Crystals: These remind one to be fair and just; to wear crystals helps in healing and in communication.

Flowers:
Sweet-Pea, Wild Rose, Clover: Gemini likes variety, and these delicate blossoms allow for many "whims." The four-leafed clover is a lucky emblem.

Tree:
Laurel: From the oak family, it has a stocky trunk and low-spreading branches. To earn a "Laurel Wreath" or "Crown of Glory" is to win the symbol of fame, honor, and divinity.

Birds:
Parrot: Its bright-colored feathers reflect beauty; it is also interesting because it possesses the ability to imitate human speech.
Myna Bird: Also a talking bird, often kept as a pet.

Animal:
Squirrel: In spite of its quick and nervous movements, it is a thrifty provider for the future, gathering food in time of plenty to save for a time of scarcity.

CANCER SYMBOLOGY

Beacon Light Upon The Shoals

The Lights from the shores shine forth beckoning, yet warning of dangerous reefs near the harbors of home. Let thy Lights be far reaching, for the sea is subtle and entreating. Cling close to faith and truth.

I Corinthians 15:41
"There is one glory of the Sun, and another glory for the Moon, and another glory of the Stars, for one star differeth from another in glory."

"Careful Cancer"
You have a strong self-image and sense of self-consciousness, which can allow you to shape both your inner soulic and outer physical natures. Your sensitivity leads to understanding and loving care for your family members, and you have a powerful need to protect and guide those in your environment. You are patriotic and personable, and you have great skills at planning and preparing. You can also be fluctuating in your emotions.

Cancer Graces:
Loyalty, self-reliance, deep thinker, intuitive.

CANCER, see **PLATE IV** for color.

Cancer Challenges:
Emotional sensitivity, shyness, secretiveness, can be moody and restless.

The Glyph: ♋ The Crab
Its hard shell hides and protects the soft interior.

The Ruling Planet: The MOON ☽
Impressionability, the personality, sub-conscious mind.

Pictured Symbology of CANCER

Gem:
Moonstone: Brings a sense of reality, warmth and love. Enhances clairvoyance, sharpens spiritual awareness and symbolizes the "Third Eye."

Flowers:
Madonna Lily, Iris, Cat-tail: Flowers of delight, symbolizing purity and majesty.

Tree:
Willow: The Bible mentions the weeping willow growing by the waters of Babylon. It gives medicinal value, and symbolizes sympathetic nuture.

Birds:
Sea Gull: A large or white sea creature that lives along the coast, clearing away and recycling things others have discarded.
Goose: Known for its precise flying formation, it refers to order and systematization. Also an excellent swimmer.

Animals:
Camel: Although it is a dry-sand traveller who goes without water for days, it is called the ship-of-the-desert and represents endurance.

8

LEO SYMBOLOGY

The Illumined Cross Above The Earth

It is only when thine eyes can look beyond the egoic radiance that the cross of roseate beauty, the Central Fire, is seen. Let the secret of thy Light reveal that the law of balance is in the vital life power which comes from the Sun. Be strong in heart in all things, and let thy faith become the ruling essence.

Psalm 121:1
"I will lift up mine eyes unto the hills from whence cometh my strength."

"Lordly Leo"
You may tap into the source of leadership for the soul which the spirit can manifest in the personality, but this must be done without assuming too great a pride and importance in the self. The desire to be at the head of situations can turn to kind assistance to others, for you know where you are going and how you are going to get there.

Leo Graces:
Honor, courage, kindness, generosity.

LEO, see **PLATE V** for color.

Leo Challenges:
Domination, vanity, egotism.

The Glyph: ♌ The Lion
Depicts the mane and tail of the lion; emblem of the Sun's fire,
Creative Force, and Cosmic Splendor.

The Ruling Planet: The SUN ☉
The individuality, will-power, vitality, ambition.

Pictured Symbology of LEO

Gem:
Topaz: Emblem of true friendship, helps to overcome anger, stress,
or tension.

Flowers:
Morning Glory: A vine with heart shaped leaves, it stands for
affection.
Sun-Flower: A noble observer, it always faces the Sun from dawn
to dusk, its blossom turning from East to West with the arc of the
Sun's rising and setting.

Tree:
Walnut: A tree highly prized for its fine-grained wood and edible
nuts, it adorns the home and gives nurture, comfort, and beauty.

Birds:
Peacock: Its iridescent plumage is an item of much pleasure and
admiration, a rainbow of beauty and pride.
Egret: A southern belle, decked with beautiful plumage and giving
much enjoyment and decoration.

Animals:
Lion: King of the beasts, it stands for royalty and power and shows
great courage but can be tamed.
Cats and all felines: Cats are delightful pets, affectionate, graceful,
and aristocratic. One special breed of domestic cat is the Siamese,
an animal of particular pride and distinction.

VIRGO SYMBOLOGY

The Growing Vine With Fronds Unfolding

From the valleys and from the hilltops the growing things of earth feed the hungering in spirit and in truth. As a light it bestows faith, honesty, and kindly healing. In its awareness it works toward fulfillment, creation, preservation, and transformation throughout endless ages.

Mark 23:11
"He that is the greatest among you, is the servant of all."

"Vigilant Virgo"
Your nature is to serve freely, with great attention to details and thoroughness in every situation. You are methodical with inborn efficiency and finish all jobs you start. You are precise, well-organized, and conscientious.

Virgo Graces:
Humanity, discrimination, fastidious.

Virgo Challenges:
Criticism, fussiness, skepticism.

VIRGO, see **PLATE VI** for color.

The Glyph: ♍ The Virgin
The virgin holds a sheaf of wheat, pure and unspoiled.

The Ruling Planets: VULCAN ⨺
Selfless service, conscience.

MERCURY ☿
Intelligence, judgment, practicality.

Pictured Symbology of VIRGO

Gem:
Zircon: A stone much favored by the ancients, it brings nobility,
emotional balance, respect, and self-esteem.

Flowers:
Orange Blossom: A very delicate blossom representing purity, it is
often used as a wreath in weddings.
Corn-flower: With its sky-blue color indicating heaven, it is a
symbol of beauty and happiness.

Tree:
Honey Locust: A favorite tree because of the beauty of its blossoms
and its many uses, including its durable wood for construction.

Birds:
Love-birds: Symbols of faith and contentment, their singing and
caressing reveals a capacity for extreme affection to their mates.
Cockatoo: A parrot-like bird, very discriminatory and fastidious in
action.

Animals:
Bear: Relates to the primal stages of growth and therefore to
instinct.
All Small Pets: Also relates to beginning stages.

10

LIBRA SYMBOLOGY

Rainbow Of Beauty And Art, Prism Of Light

As God's silvery rain fell upon the earth, it mingled with the Celestial Light and thus arose the "Birth of Color." Look ye here for the symbol of balance and truth, and be thou the artist to adorn the earth with beauty and love.

Job 31:6
>   "Let me be weighed in an even balance, that God may know mine integrity."

"Loving Libra"
Represents the point of balance between the self and the not-self where the first demands for the consideration of others are made. Peace and harmony are so important to you in life that the least vibration of discord disturbs the balance. Because you see both sides of a question so very plainly, you are often asked to mediate or judge in the problems of others.

Libra Graces:
>   Tactfulness, refinement, justice, and graciousness.

LIBRA, see **PLATE VII** for color.

Libra Challenges:
Diffidence, fickleness, fondness of flattery.

The Glyph: ♎ The Balance Scales
Signifies equilibrium and justice.

The Ruling Planet: VENUS ♀
Luxury, sociability, friendliness.

Pictured Symbology of LIBRA

Gem:
Red Coral: Coral has been used for thousands of years as a charm to protect against adverse influences, depression or temptation's urges.

Flowers:
Lupine: Stands for warmth and friendship.
Jonquil: Represents rejoicing and happiness.

Tree:
Alder: The downy yellow flower catkins of the Alder cheer the intellect and aid in literature.

Birds:
Turtle Dove: Its soft cooing indicates great affection for one's mate.
Nightingale: Its pure, sweet, bell-like song continues far into the night and suggests "prima donna" qualities.

Animals:
Hare: A vegetarian, fond of leaping and skipping, its keen hearing signifies attentiveness and a good listener.

11

SCORPIO SYMBOLOGY

Star Of Heaven And Of The Sea

Not as the eagle flieth to heights anew,
not as the scorpion hiddeth from another's view,
but as a star shineth in bright acclaim,
or as the starfish crawleth in earth's domain,
but as thy heart divineth thy spirit's rise to gain,
let not self-will defileth what faith might well attain.

I Corinthians 16: 13-14
   "Be watchful, stand firm in your faith, be courageous, be strong.
   Let all that you do be done in love."

"Strenuous Scorpio"
   Your desires are seldom found in mortal life; thus, you can be
satisfied only by attaining Oneness in spiritual consciousness.
Although many crises and dramatic events may occur, pain will
heighten your desire to understand the eternal Plan. By working to
help others, you may become a good detective, private investigator, or
government agent.

Scorpio Graces:
   Occult interest, scientific skill, theatrical talent.

SCORPIO, see **PLATE VIII** for color.

Scorpio Challenges:
Aggression, secrecy, jealousy.

The Glyph: ♏ The Scorpion
This is the only Sign with three symbols (the scorpion, the eagle, and the phoenix), which symbolizes the three parts of mind.

The Ruling Planet: PLUTO ♀
Regeneration, reform, spirituality.

Pictured Symbology of SCORPIO

Gem:
Fire Opal: Stimulates desire for greater attainment.

Flowers:
Chrysanthemum: Represents adaptability.
Geranium: Signifies active and pioneering spirit.

Tree:
Cactus: A thorny plant which grows in all shapes and sizes, giving a variety of uses—as fruit, medicine, or food.

Birds:
Eagle: The national emblem of the United States, it has sharp vision and flies extraordinarily high, thus becoming a symbol of lofty thought.
Heron: Standing straight and tall, it is a proud and skilled hunter and fisher.

Animal:
Serpent: Because of its spiral-like movement, it becomes a symbol of mankind's progression to higher goals.

12

SAGITTARIUS SYMBOLOGY

Winged Horns Of Plenty As Blessings

Thoughts of abundance stream forth as roadways for marching feet, for such is the law of goodness and truth. All good things are made possible by faith in the philosophy of Divine Law.

Proverbs 28:20
   "A faithful man shall abound with blessings."

"Prophetic Sagittarius"
   You are offered spiritual truth and your mind becomes inspired toward the growth of higher consciousness in the plane of Divine Spirit when you take the selfless course. Eager to expand horizons, you may seek to become a psychologist, philosopher, or philanthropist.

Sagittarian Graces:
   Sincerity, justice, friendliness, joviality.

Sagittarian Challenges:
   Daring, gushing, plunger or gambler.

SAGITTARIUS, see **PLATE IX** for color.

The Glyph: ↗ The Archer
  Represents the Centaur (half-horse, half-man) with an arrow pointing to the stars, indicating the conflict of instinct and wisdom.

The Ruling Planet: JUPITER ♃
  Idealism, expansiveness, generosity, abstract thinking.

Pictured Symbology of SAGITTARIUS

Gem:
  Turquoise: The turquoise is called the forget-me-not of the jewels. Its vibrations give grace, hope, and courage and its energy awakens one's pride and ability. It was valued by the American Indians for helping them get in touch with the forces of Mother Nature.

Flowers:
  Wild Pink: Reminiscent of refinement, culture, and courtesy.
  Dandelion: It represents a flirtatious nature, that gives relief of tension.

Tree:
  Cypress: Maturing slowly, it is long-lived and valuable for its endurance.

Birds:
  Swan: Signifies a graceful and fastidious nature.
  Quail or Bobwhite (a small quail): It often forms groups for mutual benefit and protection.

Animal:
  Stag: A stately animal indicating pride.

13

CAPRICORN SYMBOLOGY

The Vine Clad Rock Of Ages

Just beyond the rock-cliff walls of space rolls the sea of infinity. But the Father, knowing the limitation of the children's reaching, has caused the vines to grow within the grasp of hands, and bestows faith that they may climb and behold the view.

Proverbs 15:2
"The tongue of the wise useth knowledge aright."

"Cautious Capricorn"
You guard the secret of the soul itself, which is to be revealed only to the new initiate. Your triumph in overcoming selfishness leads to attainment of illumination and self-less-ness. The strength born of struggle and limitation builds up steadily in you so liberation may be achieved.

Capricorn Graces:
Patience, prudence, independence, convention.

Capricorn Challenges:
Extreme ambition, cold personality, inhibition, brooding nature.

CAPRICORN, see **PLATE X** for color.

The Glyph: ♑ The Seagoat
Signifies extremes of height and depth.

The Ruling Planet: SATURN ♄
Construction, limitation, caution, ambition, responsibility.

Pictured Symbology of CAPRICORN

Gem:
  Black Pearl: This gem is a sign of good luck, a symbol of dignity, and gives the wearer self-assurance.

Flowers:
  Ivy: This is a clinging vine with vibrations of fidelity, truthfulness and friendship.
  Hibiscus: Symbolizes nobility.

Tree:
  Holly: The green leaves and red berries remind one of Christmas. Holly is derived from the word "Holy," and thus represents things sacred.

Birds:
  Raven: In England there are six well cared for ravens at the Tower of London. It is said that if the ravens leave, the British Empire will fall. Thus these birds signify reliability, accountability, and a trainable nature.
  Vulture: They are fast fliers, able to soar and glide in high wide circles far beyond human vision. This signifies high goals. These birds are also protected in some states as valuable "clean-up agents."

Animal:
  Turtle: Proceeding slowly and steadily, it is usually a winner.

14

AQUARIUS SYMBOLOGY

Downpouring Of Spirit Over The Earth

The Cosmos is like a vast waterfall from which the willing hand emerges, holding the vessel aloft to catch the golden essence of truth. Faith increases through the understanding heart's receptive grace.

I Kings 3:12
"Lo, I have given thee a wise and understanding heart."

"Altruistic Aquarius"
Forerunner of the times, you are the humanitarian of the Zodiac. You seek to build your spiritual qualities and thus to become partners with the "Source" in which all hope to return through cycles of Divine order and progression.

Aquarian Graces:
Originality, inventiveness, diplomacy, altruism.

Aquarian Challenges:
Eccentricity, unconventionality, an erratic nature.

AQUARIUS, see **PLATE XI** for color.

The Glyph: ♒ The Water Bearer
Suggests waves of water or electricity, which represent the out-pouring of Divine Truth.

The Ruling Planet: URANUS ⛢
Surprise, insight, higher consciousness.

Pictured Symbology of AQUARIUS

Gem:
   Carved Ivory: Aquarians do not like to be restricted to any conventional gem, preferring to choose from the wide variety of beautiful products available. Although ivory is not a gem, it has been used as a charm or religious symbol and purports to bring good luck and success.

Flowers:
   Wisteria: It appeals to the imagination because of its ethereal beauty, and brings the nostalgia of reflective memories.
   Hydrangea: With variety in color and uniformity in growth, it sparks the imagination and the creative intellect.

Tree:
   Yucca: Stands for persistence and endurance.

Birds:
   Owl: A friendly, good neighbor, it has keen vision and seems to indulge in solemn and silent contemplation.
   Scarlet Ibis: Symbolizes a sacred quest for the unknown.

Animal:
   Flying Fish: A winged fish seeking more than can be found in its native habitat, it represents the attempt to grow from emotion to intellect.

15

PISCES SYMBOLOGY

Christ In The Mirrored Waters

In the rainbowed waters or in the quiet streams, spirit prevaileth. In the mighty currents, in the bubbling springs or deepening pools, peace abides. Within the expressions of all activities lies the duality: the God-hood of man and the brotherhood of love.

Mark 5:8
"The pure in heart shall see God."

"Poetic Pisces"
The mystic of the Zodiac, you have a deep sense of compassion and smpathy for others. Such sensitivity may bring sacrifice and dedication to humanitarian pursuits. You often seek to promote the future ideal of world brotherhood through poetry and idealistic literature.

Piscean Graces:
Sympathy, kindness, modesty.

Piscean Challenges:
Worry for the woes of the world, indecision.

PISCES, see **PLATE XII** for color.

The Glyph: ♓ The Fishes
The two fishes, swimming in opposite directions, depict opposites in experiences.

The Ruling Planet: NEPTUNE ♀
Divinity, psychic ability, mysticism, vision.

Pictured Symbology of PISCES

Gem:
  Carved Coral: Coral comes in shades of white, pink, red, and even black. It stands for reason and prudence which inspires and reassures the soul and brings calmness from stress or depression.

Flowers:
  Orchid: Exotic flowers, white or purple in color, they symbolize pomp, splendor, and stately display.
  Fern: These non-flowering plants have dust-like seeds which were formerly believed to make the wearer invisible. They represent illusion.

Trees:
  Climbing Vines (as grapes, or trumpet): The grape now comes in about a thousand varieties and thus signifies plenty. The Trumpet Vine has trumpet-shaped flowers which represent triumph.

Birds:
  Pelican: A bird who will sacrifice its own blood to nourish its young, it loves fishing and practices careful management and economy.
  Pink Flamingo: This is a bird fond of adornment and sociability.

Animal:
  Frog: The little frog's peeping is a joyous sign of early spring; the Tad-pole stands for a new beginning.

PART THREE:
FURTHER TRADITIONAL ZODIAC SYMBOLOGY

16

ADDITIONAL GEMS, FLOWERS, TREES, BIRDS, AND ANIMALS

GEMS

Gems are the highest evolutionary form of the mineral kingdom. As such they have great power to receive and retain impressions. From ancient times they have been admired and sought after as pleasures and comforts. The Egyptians, Babylonians, and Assyrians wore them as talismans or charms, believing that they protected them from adversity. Early astrologers assigned certain Gems to Zodiacal Signs.

Gems become impregnated with magnetic emanations associated with their owners and wearers. These feelings are very real, for if we believe that the gems we wear produce certain results, that belief will impress itself upon our consciousness and upon our very selves, and the effects will often manifest in our experiences.

This is why some gems carry superstitions, either negative or positive, and retain vibrations of the auras of the people who wore them. Among famous historical Gems said to have influenced their owners are the great Hope Diamond and the Koh-i-noor Diamond, which is now in the British Crown Jewels. Psychometrists and others with psychic abilities may be able to discern the feelings inherent in certain stones, either as curses or blessings.

Some gems have particular astrological significance. Researchers have linked them to certain Signs and Planets, and they are considered "lucky" or appropriate to wear according to one's Sign. Often several gems are harmonious with a given Sign. The Sun Sign gives us our gem of individuality, while the Moon Sign and the Ascendant gives us our gem of personality. It is important to realize that many lists of Gems, such as that of the Jeweler's Association, are devised by *month* and not by Sign: As previously noted, months and Signs do not exactly coincide.

Following is the Jeweler's List, which is the best known and the most popular.[1] This list runs from Month to Month.

January:	Garnet	July:	Ruby
February:	Amythest	August:	Sardonyx
March:	Bloodstone	September:	Sapphire
April:	Diamond	October:	Opal
May:	Emerald	November:	Topaz
June:	Pearl	December:	Turquoise

The Astrological list is formulated according to Sign and Symbology.

ARIES (March 21st—April 20th)
Chrysoprase: relief from anxiety, restfulness
Rock Crystal: ambition
Rose Quartz: faithful friendships, tenacity
Jacinth: romanticism, fiery nature

TAURUS (April 21st—May 21st)
Lapis Lazuli: firmness, stability
Green Jasper: protection
Peridot: contemplation, firmness

---

[1] George F. Kunz, *The Curious Love of Precious Stones* (1971) New York: Dover Publications, Inc., p.319

GEMINI   (May 22nd—June 21st)
   Crystals: healing, energy
   Beryl: concentration, intellect
   Alexandrite: beautiful change, pleasure

CANCER   (June 22nd—July 23rd)
   Carnelian: good luck, wealth
   Amber: contentment, poise
   Ruby: successful love

LEO   (July 24th—August 23rd)
   Fire Opal: strong intuition
   Moldavite: spiritual growth
   Cairngorm: honor and justice

VIRGO   (August 24th—September 23rd)
   Jasper: healing
   Sardonyx: tranquility, peace
   Hematite: status

LIBRA   (September 24th—October 23rd)
   Jade: protection, immunity, harmony
   Marcasite: order, communication
   Opal: individuality, responsibility

SCORPIO   (October 24th—November 22nd)
   Selenite: calm
   Carbuncle: safety, preservation of wealth
   Sodalite: alleviates fear, creative expression

SAGITTARIUS   (November 23rd—December 21st)
   Obsidion: physical, mental, and emotional health
   Sardius: mechanical ability, protection from fire
   Agate: strength and courage

CAPRICORN   (December 22nd—January 20th)
   Onyx: fulfillment
   Garnet: constancy, fidelity
   Jet: gain and benefit.
   Asteria: gentleness

AQUARIUS   (January 21st—February 19th)
Aquamarine: eloquence, justice
Chalcedony: good fortune
Amethyst: sincerity, ideals

PISCES   (February 20th—March 20th)
Pearl: purity, faithfulness
Labradorite: laughter, pleasure
Malachite: trust

FLOWERS

We should consider Flowers as guides between the outer world of nature and its inner, hidden meaning. We seem to sense this intuitively, for we use Flowers as gifts of love and at important moments in life like births, weddings, and solemn occasions.

Each Flower carries a numerical signature which links it to a planetary group. This signature is often five petals, as in the cases of pansies, nasturtiums, and violets. There are even more Flowers whose blooms regularly consist of six-petalled structures. These include various types of lilies, and the phrase "as white as a lily" connects those Flowers with the idea of purity—a reference to the raised consciousness that the Six-Pointed Star indicates.[2]

ARIES
Clove Pink: spiciness
Musk Rose: stimulation, amorousness
Grape Hyacinth: rejuvenation

TAURUS
White Lilac: innocence
Heliotrope: devotion, faithfulness
Honeysuckle: fidelity
Mimosa: sensitivity
Verbena: adaptable

GEMINI
Tuberose: depth of thought, sincerity
Pansy: remembrance
Lily: exotic

---

[2] Consult Chapters 5 and 7 in *Our Stars of Destiny* by Faith Javane (West Chester, PA: Whitford Press, 1988).

CANCER
Moon Flower: yearning
Lotus: forgetfulness
Fleur-de-lys: the Trinity

LEO
Acacia: immortality
Peony: pride
Marigold: heart of gold

VIRGO
Veronica: fidelity
Lupin: warmth, friendship
Stock: lasting beauty
Phlox: unanimity

LIBRA
Primrose: companionship
Fox-glove: balm for the heart
Gentian: virgin pride

SCORPIO
Fuchsia: delicacy, gentle awareness
Hollyhock: stateliness, endurance
Poppy: consolation

SAGITTARIUS
Goldenrod: adventure
Heather: enchantment
Sweet William: friendship, gallantry

CAPRICORN
Forget-me-not: true love
Snow-drop: hope
Jasmine: heavenly faith

AQUARIUS
Gardenia: refreshment
Sweet Allyssum: worth beyond beauty
Tulip: dignity

PISCES

White Orchid: purity, sacredness to the Goddesses
Narcissus: vanity
Zinnia: emblem of fidelity

TREES

"Trees are our oxygen, and nature has the power to purify and refresh us."

Flower Newhouse[3]

From the tiniest sapling to the giant redwood, trees are our friends. They provide shade and comfort and even healing, for their bark or leaves are used as medicine. And when trees are sawed into boards to frame a house, they could be seen as extending their protecting "arms" around us and adding their blessings for our security.

If you sit slightly to the right of a tree with your back to the North, you can receive messages telling the secrets of the trees. Some trees are "healing trees;" if you meditate with your back against them, your meditations will be particularly productive, and the tree may even "speak" to you.

The Trees of The Zodiac

ARIES

Red Maple: The tree that provides the makings of that delicious syrup, maple butter, and maple sugar.
Hemlock: It is useful for making leather, tannin, medicine, and ink.

TAURUS

Birch: The black birch especially produces a sweet flavor used in making 'birch beer' and other pleasant drinks.
Chestnut: It brings memories of the edible nuts and the holiday song, "chestnuts roasted in an open fire."

GEMINI

Olive Tree: Prominent in Bible times, it produces a healthful fruit and a widely useful oil. The olive branch is a symbol of peace.
Mulberry: Provides a raspberry-like fruit, favorite to both man and birds.

---

[3] Flower Newhouse, *Insights Into Reality* (1975) Escondido, CA: The Christward Ministry, pp. 137-141.

Spruce: It is much used in violin making.

CANCER

Cottonwood: It is valuable as a wind-breaker and for providing shade.

Privet: This is popular for hedges, used either for a full-height fence or for its full green leaves and white flower decorations.

LEO

Mountain Ash: A beautiful, ornamental tree, bearing bright red berries, food for both song and game birds.

Almond Tree: It produces attractive spring flowers and foliage. The nuts from this tree were sent as a gift to the Pharoah (Genesis 43:11).

VIRGO

Hazelnut: This is a cultivated tree producing an edible almond-like nut.

Tulip Tree: Its white wood is of great economic value.

LIBRA

Cherry Tree: Cultivated both for its fruit as well as for ornamentation.

Sycamore: A beautiful shade tree, it also produces a soft round nutlet, giving this tree a second name: the buttonwood.

Balsam: A Balsam tree, formerly the Balm of Giliad, provided a favorite ointment of healing (see Jeremiah 8:22).

SCORPIO

White Cedar: An evergreen with a sweet camphor-like fragrance, it is sometimes known as Arbor Vitae. It is a symbol of longevity and constancy in friendship. Other uses of Cedar include shingles and fence-posts. The Indians used this tree for their Totem Poles and dug-out canoes.

Box Elder: A member of the maple family, it is fastgrowing and strong in endurance against drought, wind, and weather. It is also a most wanted shade tree.

SAGITTARIUS

Oak: Prized by the Druids, the oak is a symbol of strength, and one of the world's more useful trees its trunk provides fine hard wood, its acorns provide food for wild-life, and its oak bark provides medicinal value.

Poplar, or Aspen: Symbol of Nature's Helper, it provides shade and quick cover for barren areas.

Fig Tree: It produces a most healthful fruit which can be eaten raw or cooked and has beautiful large leaves used as decorations. It is a symbol of the "Tree of Life" and of knowledge.

CAPRICORN

Yew Trees: Prevalent as landscaping features and often found in church yards, these trees are desired for their evergreen beauty.

Red Wood, Sequoia: They symbolize longevity.

AQUARIUS

Pomegranate: It bears large red, round, edible fruit containing many seeds and tasty flesh. It is used for flavoring and syrups.

Crab Apple: A fruit astringent, its pink and white flowers are most decorative and fragrant.

PISCES

Vines rather than trees are native to Pisces.

Quaking Aspen: Its leaves tremble almost incessantly, creating a high, soft rustle.

BIRDS

Birds are yet another blessing that Nature shares with us. Throughout the summer we can enjoy watching "our feathered friends." When we place a bird-bath or a feeding-station in our yard, we are graced with untold pleasure watching the birds gather to eat and refresh themselves each morning. Aside from contributing their varied songs for our entertainment and generally spreading good cheer, birds are also important contributors to a balanced and healthful environment, for they free our orchards from insect pests and gather countless unwanted weed-seeds from our gardens.

ARIES

Starling: full of enterprise and initiative, a symbol of aggression

Cat Bird: a busy-body, active, saucy, and inquisitive; a fighter for its needs, wants, and desires

TAURUS
Patridge: a good singer who gives interesting and lively performances
Thrush: a twittering and gentle singer with lush feathered attire

GEMINI
Pee Wee: noisy and talkative, a symbol of perpetual communication
Jay: a clever, alert, and wary sentinel
Humming Bird: a versatile and expert aviator

CANCER
Duck: expert fisherman, a good swimmer and diver
Cuckoo: shy and secretive in its habitat and work

LEO
Bird of Paradise: a symbol of pride and beauty
Golden Warbler: striking in appearance, with its magnificent colors and aureate charm

VIRGO
Chewink, or Ground Robin: a shy bird that keeps close to its home
Chick-a-Dee: friendly and helpful to neighbors, it enjoys group travel and fine dining

LIBRA
Blue Bird: dignified and meek, prefers the peacefulness of the comfortable and familiar
Boblink: pleasantly noisy and chattering

SCORPIO
Peregrine Falcon: known for great extremes in speed, a crafty hunter who always captures the prey
Phoenix: symbol of regeneration and immortality

SAGITTARIUS
Cardinal: carefree and charming and a beautiful singer
American Redstart or Firetail: restless and feverish, it is always on the go

CAPRICORN
Scarlet Tanager: often concealed by the trees while it sings its

unique and easily recognized rich melodies

Wren, Common Wren, or Jenny Wren: impatient, inquisitive, and busy, it is at times harsh and grating

Zebra-Back Woodpecker: loves the country, somewhat erratic in its movements

AQUARIUS

Oriole: artistic, thorough, and eccentric

Hawk: bold and daring in pursuit of its goals

PISCES

Snow Bird: a good planner with plenty of common sense

Mocking Bird: a versatile songster who loves to sing by the light of a full moon

ANIMALS

The Animals are considered our friends and "younger siblings" and as such should be loved, respected, and cared for. And just as we have received assistance in our evolution from caring and selfless Angelic Guardians, so, too, should we help our animal relations in *their* evolution. Indeed, Christ, whose coming revealed to us the way of our evolution, said, "The things that I do, ye may do also." Thus, the proper care of the Animal Kingdom and its habitats is one of humanity's more serious responsibilities.

"Other sheep I have which are not of this fold .... My sheep hear my voice, and I know them."

John 10:16, 27

Many humans are close to animals. Many households have cats, dogs, or other pets that are considered "part of the family." And in rural societies, people rely very much upon such farm animals as cows, horses, sheep, oxen, and pigs, all of whom have proven extremely valuable to the human communities they live in. Indeed, animals who live close to humans come to demonstrate human-like qualities.

Some people are extremely close to animals, and are able to communicate with them. The American Indians have long been noted for their harmonious co-existence with animals. The book *Kinship With All Life* is a wonderful collection of stories dealing with the

the relations between "man and beast." In the book, the man who was the caretaker of Strongheart, the famous movie dog, described the uncanny understanding of humans by animals through the use of their great powers of instinct and intelligence. In his experiences, the caretaker sought out others who had close relationships with animals, in order to understand better the link between them and people. He encountered a man living in the desert who came in constant contact with a large variety of animals, both domestic and wild. This man told the caretaker that this feeling of kinship was a "natural instinct" with most dogs. When pressed for a more specific answer, the man became silent for a long while, finally, he yawned and slowly spoke, "There's facts about dogs and there's opinions about them. The dogs have the facts, the humans have the opinions."[4] A true expert on human-animal relations had spoken!

"But ask now the beasts and they shall tell thee."

Job 12:7

We can thus learn and realize that the Divinity within all life innately relates us to every other living thing, making our connections to animals something we should cherish dearly.

Different experts perceive animals differently, and thus some disagreement may exist over the assignment of specific animals to specific Signs. Furthermore, one group of animals may be spread over several Signs. For instance, it is not likely that all of the many breeds of dogs share the same characteristics. To think of the terrier and the Great Dane, the bull-dog and the greyhound, or the Pekingese and the sleddog huskie is to realize that these diverse personalities likely fall in different Signs.

ARIES

All members of the Sheep family: firm, trustful, sensitive to others

Coyote: a clever schemer, shrewd, wary, and cautious; works better in pairs or groups

Weasel: a bold fighter, thrives on excitement, never a quitter, likes to live in the country, swift of foot

Musk Rat: a good swimmer, easily agitated, an explorer, insightful, a social climber

---

[4] J. Allen Boone, *Kinship With All Life* (1954) New York: Harper and Brothers, pp. 47-48.

TAURUS

All Cattle: symbol of physical strength

Ox: a vegetarian, patient, strong build, sturdy, resolute, conservative, dutiful

Buffolo: large, sleek, and handsome; likes trees and open country living; defensive if disturbed

Bison: a traveller and explorer with muscular shoulders and short legs

GEMINI

Monkey: charming, brilliant and inventive, ambidextrous, a fast and clever learner, likes to live among trees, often builds a 'tree house', sticks to vegetarian diet

Prairie Dog: sociable, would become a pet if tamed and trained, a good runner or racer, fast and adventurous, prefers open country living

Tiger: a delightful paradox, fun loving, a good actor, likes change and excitement, never dull

CANCER

Dog: a protector, watchful sentry, honest and likable, deeply loyal

Opossum: an amusing actor, its famous trick of 'playing possum' if attacked is a means of becoming invisible to remain unharmed; prefers to work at night

Manatee or Sea-cow: placid in temperament, likes to live lazily as if floating on calm waters; in ancient sea-lore, these were the 'mermaids,' as their habits were observed to be human-like in protecting their young

LEO

The Cat Family: hunter or pet, savage or coy, a delight

Leopard: noted for courage and valor, purveyor of elegance, symbol of royalty

Dragon: a center of energy and heroic-like power and glory; lordly, pompous, and magnificent in appearance; could be overly ambitious for success; takes love for granted; strong and vigilant and having keen eye-sight

VIRGO

Raccoon: fastidious; a stickler for cleanliness, washing all food before eating; favors night hours for work

Bear: picky eater, capable actor or worker, loves honey, mostly vegetarian, but will eat lamb or bacon if other food is not available

Praying Mantis: although religious in appearance, it is a cannibal at heart and has a ravenous appetite; has the ability to 'see' over its shoulders, which helps in gaining supplies

LIBRA

Wolf: strong personality for freedom, a kind parent, but hostile to outsiders or strangers

Fox: intelligent schemer who can live by wits alone and live well

Moose: aloof and silent, dignified in action; aggressive only if threatened, then becoming bold and challenging

SCORPIO

Beaver: an engineering genius

Fur Seal: very exclusive as to territory, will drive away any stranger who dares approach his 'harem'

Harbor Seal: neighborly and curious, it does not form 'harems' or take responsibility for others

Porcupine: unafraid and unhurried, self-sufficient and independent

Walrus: loves company and will invade groups even if dangerous to do so; has beautiful teeth

SAGITTARIUS

Antelope: a unique communicator, somewhat nervous, but very curious; has long slender legs and loves racing, and will try to overtake any passerby; sure of self and independent

Snake or Serpent: wisdom of the ages; philosopher, theologian, politician, expert financier

Giraffe: intense and selective, tall and graceful, but an awkward runner; strong, steady, purposeful for success

CAPRICORN

All members of the Goat Family:

Rocky Mountain Goat: likes to live in mountainous country

Shrew: a solitary and serious worker

Bat: radar equipped and able to use a sixth sense for finding a right direction for its purpose

Reindeer: symbol of the joyous season, likes the "limelight"

AQUARIUS

Dolphin: intelligent, understanding; has unusual talent and extraordinary eyesight: a valuable 'brother' to humanity

Rooster: herald of the day, conscious of time, precise, exact, executive

Zebra: exotic in looks, unpredictable in behavior

PISCES

Otter: playful, exuberant, all-around sportsman, especially water sports; good swimmer and diver

Ground-hog: a would-be weather prophet who has set a special day for forecasting

Boar: innocence and faith, gives freely of self; has universal goodwill, simplicity, and fortitude; is reliable and has endurance and incredible patience

17

COLORS

Rainbow of the Zodiac see **PLATE XIII** for color.

"God said, 'Let there be Light,' and there was Light."

Genesis 1:3

"LIGHT is all there is."

Walter Russell[1]

"The atom is composed of pure energy, energy is light, and light is spirit."

Annalee Skarin[2]

Color plays a great part in our lives. It brings joy, gaiety, and, when we need it, healing. Expressed through our auras, color can become an important tool in the study of self-understanding. Even common expressions like "feeling blue" or "seeing red" derive from a realization of changes in our auras, which are reflections of changes in our emotional and spiritual states.

Colors represent chemical potencies in "higher octaves" of vibration. Most color vibrations fall under twelve expressions: red, orange, yellow, green, blue-green, blue, purple, maroon, brown, gray,

[1] Walter Russell, *The Secret of Light* (1947) New York: Carnegie Hall, p. XIII.
[2] Annalee Skarin, *Ye Are Gods* (1979) U.S.A., p. 67.

or black (white is Light before it passes through a prism). Today scientists with their spectroscopes analyze the varying color of light, "taking color apart" down to the last detail. This has enabled them to examine the very nature of the universe (through study of the planets and stars), and has made the "science of vibration" valid.

The study of light and its color vibrations has a very long history. Ancient symbology incorporated universal responses to the colors. The symbolism of Egypt, China, Babylon, India, Greece, and early Christianity all recorded the same responses, which have remained constant in the following millennia.

The ancients believed that the rainbow and its colors contained the secrets of the Universe. The human body, which is ninety percent water, can act as a prism to reflect the colors of the rainbow in an aura that surrounds each person, just as a regular prism gives off the colors of the rainbow when light passes through it.

Our auras show our characteristics, personality traits and degree of evolution. Colors in our auras change with our moods, being highly sensitive to emotions like love or anger, serenity or confusion. The study of auras was an activity of some distinction in ancient times, and has recently progressed with further scientific refinements. Basically, relaxed auras contain the primary color blends, red, yellow, and blue. Red represents the physical plane of being (health, friendship, etc.); yellow represents the intellectual status; and blue represents spiritual devotion and related sentiments.

Related to auras is the value of colors for healing. Colors can produce important healing vibrations, which often depend upon the color preferences of the individual. A helpful adjunct to these color vibrations is the healing power of music, for the tones of the musical scale produce colors. Science has grown convinced of the tremendous effect of color upon health and healing. Further research is essential, and should teach us even more about the benefits of color.

Each of us has a favorite color compatible with our nature. These preferences can tell us something about our personality type.

If you like RED:
> Your interest in life is directed outward. You belong in the midst of life; you like action. You feel that life is meant to be happy and you get upset when it is not. You can have deep sympathies or you can be abrupt and careless.

Red has more associations and symbolism than any other color. It can signify both love and hate, virtue and evil, sacrifice and cruelty;

it is a sign of blood and fire as well as of strength, vigor, and courage.

If you like PINK:
You are charming and warm, loving and affectionate in nature, but are not extreme (for pink qualities are gentler manifestations of red qualities). You may enjoy financial advantages, or either a sheltered life or social tendencies.

If you like ORANGE:
You are social by nature and get along with all (orange qualities being equally luminous with red qualities). You have a cheerful spirit, an easy smile, and ready conversation, and you do not like to be alone.

If you like YELLOW:
Intellectual and idealistic, you have orderly habits in thinking and action. You are confident, develop a good philosophy to live by, and are careful not to offend others. You like things modern.

If you like GREEN:
You are a good citizen, civic-minded and moral but not prudish. Balanced and normal, value good education, and tend to be prosperous.

If you like BLUE-GREEN (AQUAMARINE, TURQUOISE):
You are discriminating and fastidious, neat, well-groomed, and sharp-witted. You need to be loved, rather than to love. You have a sensitive nature and value tranquility, refinement, and culture. You manage your own affairs well, and do not lean on others.

If you like BLUE:
Wealth, social standing, respect, and sensitivity to others are among your many qualities. You are modest in dress and action. A loyal friend, you would make a good student, executive, or healing worker. Blue is the most preferred color and has a universal appeal.

If you like PURPLE (VIOLET):
Powerful and healing, you are philosophical but may lack perseverance. You are idealistic and often artistic. Purple is an enigmatic color suggesting exclusiveness and is seldom identified with the mundane.

If you like BROWN:
Strong and steady, you are a conscientious, conservative person who seeks to attend to the duties of established habits rather than change by pressures from others. You are dependable, reliable, and honest, but you know how to make a good bargain in business.

If you like GRAY:
You are cautious and practical and want to be of service to others. Quiet and unobtrusive, you wish to live in peace and have usually acquired wisdom.

If you like BLACK and WHITE:
You are sophisticated and dignified, tend to engage in creative activity, and often value inner qualities over outer show. The black and white combination—the presence and absence of color, all color and no color—symbolizes purity and both polarity and balance. This is a combination that is attractive and becoming to almost everyone.

These colors are also associated with the Zodiacal Signs.

ARIES
Red: "Colors" and gives tone to the muscles. Indicates that your attention focuses innately on what surrounds you, and your outlook on life is optimistic.

TAURUS
Emerald Green: Representing the universal attraction of nature, this gives a soothing and revitalizing vibration.

GEMINI
Yellow: Reveals an idealistic drive towards self-fulfillment, an intellectual nature, and the development of a unique philosophy of life.

CANCER
Pastels, Iridescent Blues: Colors of universal appeal, and of preference which increases in proportion to education and income, they mark loyal friends and good students.

LEO

Orange and Gold: Orange indicates a cheerful and social nature and existence in harmony with others. Gold, a brilliant and valuable metal, represents the Gold Medal, the prize of honor.

VIRGO

Violet: Helpful to the nervous system, brain and eyes, often used in healing.

LIBRA

Green (all shades), Autumn Yellow, and Gold: Green stands for creative activity. Yellow and Gold are healing colors, and Golden Yellow signifies wisdom. Green is helpful to the glandular system and for heart and circulatory conditions; Yellow and Gold work to benefit the spinal nervous system, lungs, and kidneys. The Libra combination of colors brings balance and harmony to the total person.

SCORPIO

Scarlet: Represents abstract ideals.

SAGITTARIUS

Royal Red, Royal Blue: These colors stand for wisdom and devotion to ideals.

CAPRICORN

Indigo, Navy Blue: Indigo promotes religious feelings, tranquility, and peace, and commands respect. Navy blue denotes loyalty and conservatism.

AQUARIUS

Electric Blue, Opalescence: Electric Blue relates to the will and to dedication. Opalescence indicates an aesthetic effect giving a peculiar significance to brilliant gems.

PISCES

Silvery White, Sea Green: Silvery White impresses with a sense of power and of purity in thought. Sea Green denotes creative activity, strong spiritual influence, and a zeal for truth.

18

MUSIC

"Music is a part of the beauty of the spirit."

"Music may span the space between finite and infinite, in harmony
of sound, in harmony of color—even in harmony of motion itself—
all beauty is akin to the soul-self's expression of harmony in the
mind."

Edgar Cayce[1]

An ancient sage once observed that the spiritualization of matter is
accomplished by means of sound. Indeed, music is often called a
universal language, for it resonates with the emotions that we all
experience and relate to. Music is perhaps humanity's supreme
expression of the emotions, communicating feelings of hope, joy,
rapture, peace, or ecstasy, or of fury, fear, hostility, tragedy, or
sorrow.

Because music is a universal emanation, it relates closely to other
physical phenomena, including motion and color. Indeed, tones of the
musical scale produce colors, and both color and tones carry great
latent power. Melody appeals to the higher spiritual centers, and the
power of rhythm appeals to the lower physical centers.

[1] Edgar Cayce, Readings 3659-1

The powers inherent in music have the great ability to re-align us to our truer centers and thus to heal us of various negative life experiences. The physical body, like a musical instrument, is attuned to a particular frequency. This frequency will vibrate within the individual and also into the surrounding atmosphere, into regions both internal and external that have strong connections with the healing of the body, the mind, the spirit, and the emotions.

Music has long been recognized for these qualities. It was used for its healing powers in the Sacred Temples of Egypt. There, the priests used chants and prayers to calm restless souls. And the great seer and therapist Paracelsus practiced what he called "musical medicine," telling his followers that certain melodies would be beneficial in combatting their illnesses.

Relief from disease through music comes as the body is raised and strengthened. Different types of music and different instrumental combinations are used for different types of trouble. For example, some bright music with strong rhythmic pulsations makes people feel intensely alive and wanting to dance and spin around and whirl. Such activity can be a valuable outlet for inner pressures such as depression or nervousness. Or quieter music may serve to soothe people and thus promote well-being.

Instrumental music is usually more effective than vocal music in healing, for with instruments fewer personal elements enter into treatment. For example, wood instruments, with their peculiarly penetrating tone, seem to help the more nervous. However, research has found that within vocal music, the soprano voice does help improve people with cases of acute melancholia, while the tenor voice assists in the treatment of brain disease and the baritone voice best serves paranoiacs.

Because of the emotional nature of music, each individual will respond best to a different musical style or instrumentation. To hear the particular music one enjoys can tune an individual in to a healing, soothing rhythm of transcendence that can lift the consciousness to a realm of inner peace. This individualized approach is the key to effective healing through music.

Along with responding to the healing powers of a particular sort of music, each individual also has his or her own "Key Note." Every created being from molecule to humanity, from every plant to the Solar System, possesses a Key Note of its own. You can discover your own Key Note by listening to the tone of your voice. Go to a piano and speak in your most natural tone. Strike notes as close as possible to the caliber of your voice; strike above, strike below until your voice matches, or vibrates in accord with, a particular note. This is your Key Note, or "Soul Note," which you may hum or sing until your whole being seems to vibrate to it, to stimulate your spiritual awareness, health, and further growth. The Note's harmonics produce a spiralling, fiery energy of positive influence in your life, stimulating your aura and flowing along the spine, sometimes entering the throat chakra and thus inspiring you to sing.

These individual aspects of music help attune the individual to the power of the Universe. Thus music can be a great and positive force in the search to understand the mysteries of life. It should therefore come as little surprise that music can be related to the Horoscope. Each Sign is best represented by a particular sort of music. A brief description of each sort follows, along with several pieces that exemplify each Sign.

ARIES music is dynamic and strong, with great chords, and is often martial in flavor. Examples: Stars And Stripes Forever (Sousa), Prelude in C# Major (Rachmaninoff).

TAURUS music has feeling, is often lush and meditative, yet can often also be vibrant and earthy. Examples: Meditation from Thais (Massenet), Tales Of The Vienna Woods and other waltzes (Strauss).

GEMINI music is bright and cheerful, often intellectual, and logical and thematic with intricate compositional and variational processes. Examples: Falling Leaves Reverie in Eb (Mueller), Anitra's Dance (Grieg), Album Leaf (Wagner).

CANCER music is the music of nature and of the people, including folk tunes and dances. Examples: Country Gardens (Grainger), To A Wild Rose (MacDowell), Clair de Lune (Debussy).

LEO music is vital and powerful. Examples: Hymn to the Sun (Rimsky-Korsakoff), Finlandia (Sibelius), Polish Dance (Scharwenka).

VIRGO music is pure, systematic, and meticulous, and often devotional. Examples: Minuet (Paderewsky), Idilio (Lack), Humoresque (Dvorak).

LIBRA music expresses love and harmony. Examples: Liebestraum (Liszt), The Swan (Saint-Saens), Evening Star (Wagner).

SCORPIO music is sensational, keen, sharp, often piercing to the very heart of reality. Examples: Danse Macabre (Saint-Saens), Valse Triste (Sibelius), Violin Concerto (Brahms).

SAGITTARIUS music is music of the higher mind, involving ideas and comtemplation, and emotion stirred in an abstract way. Examples: Moonlight Sonata (Beethoven), Rhapsody In Blue (Gershwin), Polonaises (Chopin).

CAPRICORN music is quite sedate in style. Examples: Largo (Dvorak), In The Hall Of The Mountain Kings (Grieg), The Rosary (Nevin).

AQUARIUS music is music of unusual melodies that seems to penetrate all space. Examples: Bolero (Ravel), Malaguena (Albeniz), Skater's Waltz (Waldteufel).

PISCES music is impressionistic, imaginative, everchanging, and suggestive of the greater life of the spirit. Examples: Ave Maria (Schubert), Semper Fidelis (Sousa), Sweet Mystery Of Life (Herbert).

19

INCENSE

Incense, and related perfumes and elixirs, touch our consciousness via our sense of smell. The sense of smell varies among people, but it can be trained: for example, pharmacists and physicians can tell drugs or diseases by odor. Odors fix themselves in the memory, and places and events can be recalled after many years by association with a particular odor. Certain odors can even stimulate emotional response, which in turn can influence physical character and health. Odors also affect the mental and even spiritual side of people through the discriminatory power of the sense of smell, for it is only the subtle or psychic abilities that can perceive the finer vibrations in nature. Incense thus has the capacity to stimulate our development on many levels.

Incense has a long history of usage, and from the start this usage has been closely linked with spiritual affairs. Records mentioning the use of incense occur in ancient Egypt as early as 3580 B.C. There, it was burnt to the Sun daily. Aside from its use as an offering, it was used mainly for prayer and meditation, with the Egyptians believing that the rising smoke carried praise and petitions to the gods. Incense was also used in embalming, for funerals, to honor the Pharaohs, and in various other religious ceremonies.

The use of incense has been as universal as it has been longstanding. The Old Testament includes numerous mentions of anointing oils, incense, and holy perfumes. We read of the anointing of Kings and of the Ark of the Covenant, of altars of burnt offerings and of fragrant incense, and of scented candle-sticks and sacred vessels.

India also used many exotic incenses, on garments as well as in fires for marriage ceremonies and funerals. The Chinese used incense widely in their temples, as did the Japanese, who also enjoyed incense in the home. In Arab lands, which provided many of the fragrant herbs and aromatic gums that comprise incense, great mystery surrounded the making of incense and perfume. In the construction of several mosques, the mortar was even mixed with a large quantity of musk so that the buildings would emit sweet odors when the sun shone on them.

The ancient Greeks believed that perfumes were of Divine origin. Theophrastus, the "Father of Botany," studied the odors produced uniquely by each plant, knowledge that helped the Greeks prepare concoctions that lasted for unusually long periods of time. And in ancient Mexico, incense was used in the great public processions and festivals of the Aztecs.

Christians began using incense in the fourth century, in the catacombs of Rome. It gradually came into general use, and became an important facet of the rituals of the Catholic Church.

An examination of this ancient and widespread usage of incense reveals that not only did most societies employ incense in their religious rites, but that incense had important medicinal applications as well. Many peoples understood the antiseptic properties of the gums, resins, and other essences used, and burnt incense for the physical as well as spiritual purification of the people as well as for repelling disease. These mixes were also taken internally as elixirs in order to cleanse the body. These healing incenses and elixirs are the result of painstaking, detailed study, and consist of complicated combinations of flowers, spices, fruits, herbs, gums, resins, vegetables, roots, barks, and even minerals and gems. Thus can incense become an important tool for the cultivation of one's physical, mental, and spiritual well-being and progress.

As well as its connection to religious ceremony and to healing, incense has often been connected with the art of Astrology. The ancients classified the sources of scents and gave to the Signs and Planets rulerships over all aromatic substances. This Astrological knowledge has proven an effective basis on which to organize the powers and influences that incense can have upon us.

ARIES   carnation, cedar, frankincense, myrrh, pine

TAURUS   benzoin, rose, saffron, sandalwood

GEMINI   citron, clover, lavender, mace, mastic

CANCER   gardenia, lemon, lotus, red storax, rose, violet

LEO   frankincense, juniper berries, mastic, orange blossom, sandalwood

VIRGO   cypress, lavender, mace, patchouli, sandalwood

LIBRA   lilac oil, marjoram, sandalwood, sweet pea, thyme, violet

SCORPIO   allspice, frankincense, ginger, opopanax, pine

SAGITTARIUS carnation, clover, frankincense, lignum aloes, myrrh, sage

CAPRICORN   cypress, patchouli, sandalwood, violet

AQUARIUS   acacia, cypress, euphorbium, mastic, pine, sandalwood

PISCES   eucalyptus, frankincense, gardenia, sarsaparilla

20

HEALING HERBS AND THE BODY

"He causeth the grass to grow for cattle and herbs for the use of man."

Psalm 104:14

The use of herbs in healing signifies a belief that nature provides for our every need, and in due season, for the creation of better health and a better life.

"And the fruit thereof shall be for meat, and the leaf thereof for medicine."

Ezekiel 47:12

An effective use of herbs for healing is based upon genuine need and a sincere faith in their power. The power of herbs is in the life essence, the *substance* of all that lives. This has long been recognized, and for thousands of years healers have studied the properties of herbs and other plants to derive remedies for the diseases that afflict humanity. Many commonly-used foodstuffs are of medicinal value, including onions, apples, cashews, rice, lettuce, garlic, and parsley. And throughout the Earth's vast gardens grow many more common-place *and* exotic herbs that are important aids in the healing arts.

Any use of herbs for healing is best undertaken under the guidance of a sympathetic physician or an herbalist. Many herbs are specifically related to certain parts of the body, and are most effective healing agents when these parts are diseased. These herbs, and their respective body parts, are also attuned to our Zodiacal Signs.

ARIES
Body Part: the Head, the Face
Related Conditions: headache, toothache, other head ailments, fevers
Healing Herbs: barberry, burdock, clove, ginger (also believed to bring money and good luck), hops (good for sleeplessness), mustard, rhubarb, nettles, sweetbriar

TAURUS
Body Part: the Throat, the Neck
Related Conditions: sore throat, goiter, excessive eating or drinking, emotional upset
Healing Herbs: pennyroyal, peppermint, plantain, sage (produces a calming and soothing effect), tansy, thyme (restores courage), vervain

GEMINI
Body Part: the Arms, the Lungs, the Nervous System
Related Conditions: nervousness, respiratory ills
Healing Herbs: anise, caraway, fern, lung-wort, mandrake, parsley (a blood purifier and nervine, also relieves worry), skullcap, valerian

CANCER
Body Parts: the Chest, the Stomach
Related Conditions: indigestion, dropsy, asthma, cancer, pleurisy
Healing Herbs: black hellebore, catnip, chickweed, honeysuckle (leaves only), Indian poke, lettuce (for equalizing the emotions), mace, wintergreen

LEO
Body Parts: the Heart, the Spine
Related Conditions: circulatory ailments, problems of general health
Healing Herbs: angelica, balm, eyebright, ginger, lavender, marigold, mistletoe, rosemary, rue, saffron, St. John's wort,

wake-robin, walnut (an excellent all-around food, should be part of every salad)

VIRGO
Body Part: the Digestive System, the Liver (on which the health of the whole body depends; the physical center of responsibility)
Related Conditions: dysentery, colic, gastritis, appendicitis
Healing Herbs: althea, dill (for cleansing), fennel (for cleansing), licorice (purifies the blood), marjoram, marsh-mallow, plantain, skullcap (tones the system), valerian

LIBRA
Body Parts: the Back (lumbar region), the Kidneys
Related Conditions: inflammation of kidney and bladder, back pain, blood disease
Healing Herbs: absinthe, archangel, artichoke, balm, burdock, catmint, mullein, leeks, parsley, pennyroyal (warm and soothing, can be used by many people of other Birth-Signs), silver-weed, violet, wild thyme

SCORPIO
Body Parts: the Generative Organs
Related Conditions: hemorrhoids, ruptures
Healing Herbs: blessed thistle, capers, hops, horehound (cleansing and antiseptic), horse-radish, leek, sarsaparilla, spotted thistle, wormwood

SAGITTARIUS
Body Parts: the Thighs, the Organs of Locomotion (the Sacral region)
Related Conditions: rheumatism and neuritis in the lower limbs
Healing Herbs: chicory, dandelion, Indian hemp, liver wort, maiden fern, oak tree bark (a fine astringent, also processed and used in massage), red clover, sage, thorn apple

CAPRICORN
Body Parts: the Bones, the Knees
Related Conditions: rheumatism, rickets, fractures, skin diseases, warts
Healing Herbs: comfrey root (used fresh to make an ointment for warts), fig-wort, flax seed, heal-all, knot grass, mullein, plantain, sheperd's purse, slippery elm, wintergreen, wood-sage

AQUARIUS
Body Parts: the Ankles, the Calves
Related Conditions: leg cramps, paralysis, blood impurities
Healing Herbs: bayberry, comfrey, sage, snake root (for vibrancy), southernwood, spotted plantain (use in a tea), valerian, also the herbs of the Sign LEO

PISCES
Body Parts: the Feet (symbolic of understanding, illumination, and idealism)
Related Conditions: gout, boils, ulcers, abscesses, corns, lameness
Healing Herbs: cayenne, eucalyptus, Irish moss, mushrooms, seaweed, most sea plants and plants grown under water

CONCLUSION

"O Lord, our Lord, how excellent is thy name in all the earth! who has set thy glory above the heavens ... the Moon and the Stars, which thou has ordained ...."

Psalm 8:1, 3

In over fifty years of study and research, I have noticed more and more the relationship of all things to each other. This book has presented the fruits of some of my research: the relationship between Astrology and Symbology, and the relationship between the resulting knowledge and our lives and destinies.

All the inhabitants of this Earth—from animals and birds to flowers, trees, and herbs and even gems—all relate to the characteristics, challenges, and promises available to humanity and expressed in our Astrological Charts.

I have selected just a few of the many symbolic interconnections that a study of metaphysics can reveal. Perhaps this book will inspire its readers to delve more deeply into such study. Those who do will discover further confirmation of the One-ness of All Things. Light Energy, Consciousness, the Will-to-Good, God—all these are ultimately one, and all the symbolic manifestations of the earth plane find Union in them.

My blessings to you in your search for that Sacred Union!

APPENDIX A: GLYPHS

Like all Symbols, Glyphs can lead those who study them toward the wonder of knowledge and the truth. By learning the specific principles that underlie the Glyphs, we can derive a deeper understanding of ourselves and our place in the Universe. But because each Glyph is a Symbol of inner creative force, we may respond to them not only according to their static meaning but also according to our particular state of mind at the moment of contemplation.

ZODIACAL GLYPHS

The Zodiacal Glyphs are constructed from combinations of three basic hieroglyphs ("hiero" means "sacred" and "glyph" means "pictograph"). They are the circle, the crescent, and the line.

The line represents self-consciousness, the physical world, the flesh, and form. A vertical line stands for man or the masculine principle; a horizontal line stands for the "fallen man," one fallen in consciousness. A combination of the horizontal and vertical lines becomes a Cross, symbol for the conscious mind.

The crescent stands for our subconscious or emotional reactions. It represents the Moon (Satellite of Earth) when in New-Moon position.

The circle represents the Super-Conscious mind, and the higher plane. It symbolizes Divine Source, or God, throughout the world, for its form is without beginning or end. When it contains a central dot, it stands for the Sun. When it encloses a Cross, it represents the Planet Earth, signifying matter clothed in the garment of Spirit.

An understanding of the relationships of these three symbols in combination provide a key for interpreting the inner meanings of the Zodiacal Glyphs.

MERCURY

☿   Crescent over Circle over Cross

The union of all three symbols represents the equilibrium of all three planes of consciousness. Subconsciousness at the top shows that it is purified and up-lifted to receive inspiration and spiritual wisdom. The Cross below symbolizes self-consciousness at work adjusting personal life and physical environment. Super-consciousness in the center supports the receptive power and sends wisdom to the self-conscious plane. Thus, Mercury helps us assimilate all our earthly experiences and adjusts conflicts between inner and outer experiences—which is the challenge of life on the physical plane. Because this influence works to perpetuate human evolution, Mercury, even though it is one of the smallest planets in size, may indeed be considered the greatest of them all.

VENUS

♀   Circle over Cross

This indicates Spirit triumphant over matter, for the Cross of self-consciousness is subordinate to the Circle of Super-Consciousness. Venus is often called "The Star of Love," and its mission is to spread the principle of Love through the Cross of Matter. The Spirit of Christ, who taught, "Love ye one another even as I have loved you," emanates from Venus. Venus symbolizes the creative and artistic forces in our lives, to the extent that Super consciousness dominates our activity, with self-consciousness as its instrument.

MARS

♂   ♂   Cross over Circle

This denotes Spirit limited by matter, the "animal-man" state where self-consciousness dominates Super-Consciousness. Mars represents desire and finds expression in action and experience, energy and generation. Without this force in the world, we would be listless, without energy or Spirit or will-power. When desire is directed constructively, Mars provides the energy we need to progress, to promote good over evil, and to turn our energies and will toward the creation of our spiritual selves—thus turning generation into re-generation.

JUPITER

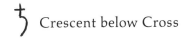 Crescent over Cross

This Glyph represents the soul liberating itself from matter. Jupiter is our guide to spiritual understanding of the True Wisdom which is beyond intellect. Its mission is to inspire with Hope, and to bring peace within through brotherhood. Jupiter is our great benefic, symbolizing philosophy, philanthropy, and the higher mind and bestowing success and good judgment.

SATURN

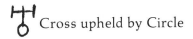 Crescent below Cross

This Glyph indicates the domination of the conscious mind over the intuitive soul-mind. It is confronted with limitations of earthly life, which requires patience, discretion, honesty, and labor, as well as humility to learn the secret of Saturn's mission. Saturn is the guardian of the inner worlds, and teaches us that human nature must become Divine, a lesson we usually learn only in our hours of trial. We must remember that wisdom is born of pain, and thus that "Saturn the task-master" is a friend in disguise, who brings Light to our souls in our darkest hours.

URANUS

Cross upheld by Circle

This denotes a raised consciousness. Uranus, the higher octave of Mercury, is called "The Awakener," and brings unexpected changes and surprise, thus challenging us to overcome difficulties through learned patience and wisdom. The mission of Uranus is to make us realize that the God within is our only source and security.

NEPTUNE

♆ Crescent over Cross

This Glyph shows the Crescent completely raised over the Cross, the crescent "cup" in the position of receptivity above the Cross of matter. The Glyph is also the Trident, the "Wand of Power" over the seas, or emotions. This combination of symbols indicated divinity. Neptune represents sympathy and influences moods, dreams, intuitions, premonitions, and visions.

PLUTO

♀ Circle over Crescent over Cross

This Glyph—the Circle of Spirit above the Crescent of Soul, both above the Cross of matter—signifies the urges of the body and the desires of the Soul under the dominance of the Spirit's will. Pluto, a higher octave of Mars, will promote idealism and the realization of Divine, transcending faith that embraces Truth and Love. These ideals will not be fully understood—and may even seem to bring trouble and testing—until humanity recognizes the inter-dependence of all and cooperates to create more universal outlooks and realities.

VULCAN

⚊ Trinity

Vulcan, thought to rule Virgo, has taken its place in our Zodiac as representing the value of self-less service. In each Horoscope, Vulcan is always close to the Sun and operates through the Birth Sign. Revolving between the Sun and Mercury, it links the mind and the Spirit, bringing out the best possible ideals from within us. It stands for that conscience which allows us to stand on our convictions and to render self-less service.

NUMERICAL GLYPHS

ONE

1 The upright line stands for unity, the masculine principle. It is the first in a series, the conscious mind, and the true "I AM" of all humanity.

TWO

2 The crescent over the horizontal line represents the soul entering matter to help raise consciousness. It denotes the feminine principle, the beginnings of division, the concept of duality. The soul is subject to matter, but the Divine feminine also stands for "the power behind the throne." Here is born the polarity by which we can become complete in unity.

THREE

3 The two crescents depict the world of expansion, creation, formation, and emanation. The three primary colors are thus seen as radiations of the Trinity, and the equilateral triangle as in formation arising from the threefold nature of the individual: body, soul, and spirit.

FOUR

4 Combining the cross and the triangle, this is a particularly sacred number, representing the four Elements, the four fixed Signs, and the four rivers (or spiritual forces) which flowed out of Eden. Many Gods also had four-letter names, including Isis, Deus, Odin, Gott, Zeus, Atma, Jove, Ptah, and I-H-V-H (Johovah).

FIVE

5 Two lines upheld by the crescent represents both the soul and the individual reaching through the powers of the five developed senses for experience. This is the symbol of change, and of working for regeneration. "It doth not yet appear what we shall be."

SIX

6 The circle upholding the line pertains to the interrelationship of the individual and desire—of the person upheld by higher consciousness, of physical love transmuted to love of the Divinity found within the self. This Glyph stands for the head and heart interlocked, for the soul quality which results from the practice of right and justice.

SEVEN

7 This is a mystic symbol of spiritual realization, of resting to attain a higher, more perfected rhythm and order. It combines the symbology and meaning of 3 (triangle) and 4 (the cube), revealing the purified body, illumined mind, and glorified spirit all prepared for higher fields of endeavor, and the eternal self developed through the forces of spiritual, physical, mental, and emotional control.

EIGHT

8 This is the number of a regenerative vibration that represents the exodus from bondage to the Promised Land of the New Age. On its side, the 8 become the lemniscate, ∞, the symbol for infinity, and the eternal spiralling motion of evolution.

NINE

9 The circle above the line shows the dominance of spiritual consciousness over self-consciousness. It governs the evolution of humanity through passion to compassion, to universal humanitarian love.

BIBLIOGRAPHY

Arguelles, Jose. *The Mayan Factor.* (1987) Santa Fe, NM, Bear & Co.
_____. *Earth Ascending.* (1988) Santa Fe, NM, Bear & Co.
_____. *Surfers Of The Zuvuya.* (1988) Santa Fe, NM, Bear & Co.
Baker, Aleta B. *She The Woman Man.* (1935) Boston, MA.
Boone, J. Allen. *Kinship With All Life.* (1954) New York, Harper & Brothers Publishers.
Bonewitz, R. A. *Cosmic Crystals.* (1983) Great Britain, Turnstone Press.
Carey-Perry, Inez Eudora. *The Zodiac And The Salts Of Salvation.* (1932), Los Angeles, CA: Carey-Perry School Of The Chemistry Of Life.
Cirlot, J. E. *A Dictionary Of Symbols.* (1962) New York, Philosophical Library.
Clark, Glenn. *The Man Who Talked With The Flowers.* (1939) St. Paul, MN: Alester Park Pub. Co.
_____. *The Man Who Tapped The Secrets Of The Universe.* (1965) Swananoa, VA: University Of Science And Philsophy.
Davidson, Donald. *Astrology.* (1963) New York: Arc Books, Inc.
Friend, Hilderic. *Flower Lore.* (1981) Rockport, MA: Para Research Inc.
Harvey, Jane. *Wildflowers Of America.* (1932) Racine, WI: Whitman Pub. Co.
Hausman, Leon A. *Field Book Of Eastern Birds.* (1946) New York: G. P. Putnam's Sons.
Javane, Faith. *Our Stars Of Destiny.* (1988) West Chester, PA: Whitford Press.

Jeans, Sir James. *The Stars In Their Courses.* (1931) New York: The Macmillan Co.

King, Julius. *Talking Leaves.* (1934) Cleveland, OH: The Harter Pub. Co.

Kunz, George F. *The Curious Lore Of Precious Stones.* (1971) New York: Dover Publications Inc.

Libra, C. Aq. *Astrology, Its Technics and Ethics.* (1917) Amersfoort, The Netherlands: P. Dz. Veen Publisher.

Lindsay, Jack. *Origins Of Astrology.* (1971) London: Frederick Muller.

Mitton, Jacqueline. *Astronomy.* (1978) New York: Charles Scribner's Sons.

Moore, Marcia and Douglas, Mark. *Astrology, The Divine Science.* (1971) York Harbor, ME: Arcane Publications.

Newhouse, Flower. *Insights Into Reality.* (1975) Escondido, CA: The Christward Ministry.

Parchment, S. R. *Astrology, Mundane and Spiritua 1.* (1933) San Francisco, CA: Rosicrucian Anthroposophic League.

Peatie, Donald C. *Trees You Want To Know.* (1934) Racine, WI: Whitman Publishing Co.

Russell, Walter. *The Secret Of Light.* (1947) New York: Carnegie Hall.

Sepharial, *The Science of Foreknowledge.* (1967) Mokelumne Hill, CA: Health Research.

Schiffer, Nancy. *The Power Of Jewelry.* (1988) West Chester, PA: Schiffer Publishing Ltd.

Skarin, Annalee. *Ye Are Gods.* (1952) New York: Philosophical Library.

Stevens, G. A. *Garden Flowers In Color.* (1933) New York: The Macmillan Co.

White, W.B. *Seeing Stars.* (1935) Harter Publishing CO.

Zim, Hubert S. and Baker, Robert H. *Stars, A Guide To The Constellations.* (1951) New York: Golden Press.

Zim, Hubert S. and Gabrielson, Ira N. *Birds, A Guide To Most Familiar American Birds.* (1956) New York: Golden Press, Western Publishing Co. Inc.

Zim, Hubert S. and Martin, Alexander C. *Trees, A Guide To Familiar American Trees.* (1956) New York: Golden Press, Western Publishing Co. Inc.

Zim, Hubert S., and Robbins, Chandler S., and Bertel, Bruun. *Birds Of North America.* (1966) New York: Golden Press, Western Publishing Co. Inc.

The Bible, King James Version.

The Forgotten Books of Eden. Rutherford H. Platt, Jr., ed. (1927) New York: Alpha House Inc.